The Peace Table

Mary Da Prato, AMI Diploma

Illustrations by Genevieve DeVaney Da Prato and Mary Da Prato
Images and text are copyrighted and may not be reproduced.

ISBN: 1507613873
ISBN-13: 978-1507613870

Table of Contents

The Peace Table

Mary Da Prato

Introduction

What is Montessori?

The Montessori Method of education, developed by Dr. Maria Montessori in 1907, emphasizes freedom of movement and work choice in a mixed-age classroom during a three hour uninterrupted time block under the guidance of a trained Montessori teacher in accordance with universal laws of human development. For more than one hundred years on every inhabited continent, Montessori's scientific and humanitarian pedagogy of guiding each individual child to his fullest potential has endured.

Dr. Montessori founded Association Montessori Internationale (AMI) in 1929 to preserve the high standards of her scientific method. This publication reflects the author's AMI Primary training. There are other Montessori training courses such as AMS (American Montessori Society), PAMS (Pan American Montessori Society), and St. Nicholas, but this publication focuses on the original Montessori Method of education as founded by Dr. Maria Montessori herself as presented to the author via oral tradition by an AMI teacher trainer.

For more information about the Montessori Method, consult the writings of Dr. Maria Montessori as well as contemporary titles including *Montessori for You and Your Child* by Mary Da Prato.

About this Book

The Peace Table is based upon Montessori conflict resolution practices introduced and reinforced in the Montessori Primary prepared environment for three through six year old children. In an unsettled world full of conflict and unrest, Montessori peace education is needed now more than ever. This book describes a holistic approach to peaceful conflict resolution and diplomacy techniques presented in the Montessori Casa, or classroom for three through six year old students, as well as essential prerequisite skills for achieving internal and external harmony as precursors to peace. It is my sincere hope that this publication will help clarify peace-centered education for children, parents, and teachers to create a harmonious world for all that fosters and embraces the best in each individual and humanity as a whole to achieve the ultimate goal of world peace.

What is The Peace Table?

The Peace Table, the inspiration for the title of this book, is a place in the Casa where three through six year old students can peaceably resolve their disputes independently or with the limited aid of an adult mediator. Setup for The Peace Table is simple. A child-sized table, two child-sized chairs, and an object symbolic of peace, such as a dove figurine or olive branch, are the only objects required to create The Peace Table. During a dispute between two students, the children sit facing one another at the same table. The object symbolic of peace acts as an inanimate mediator. The child who is holding the object speaks uninterrupted. The child who is not holding the object listens silently while the other child tells his side of the story. When the first child is finished telling his perspective, he hands the object to the other child. It is now the second child's turn to speak and the first child's turn to listen silently. The object is passed back and forth between the two children until the disagreement between them is resolved. At first, this simple turn-taking system may require help from an adult. Over time, adult help should become less necessary as students' verbal communication skills and independence blossom. Eventually, all children in the Casa should be able to resolve their disagreements independently or with minimal adult guidance. The prepared environment, a prerequisite to implementing The Peace Table effectively, is outlined in the text as a reference for parents and teachers.

Disclaimers

In this publication, parents, guides, and assistants are referred to as "she," while students are called "he." These designations, assigned for the reader's convenience, in no way reflect the gender dynamic of parents, teachers, and students in a Montessori environment.

The Peace Table does not guarantee successful conflict resolution. Attaining peaceful conflict resolution and lasting peace is an ongoing process of negotiation.

Part 1

The Foundations of Peace

The Prepared Environment

Peace begins with the prepared environment. A prepared environment for young children is defined as one that has the complete array of official Montessori Primary manipulatives,[1] a developmentally appropriate mixed-age group of students,[2] and a trained Montessori guide.[3] These three elements combined with student freedom of choice within natural limits create an optimal environment that supports every child's individual and social development to achieve the ultimate goals of internal and external peace.[4]

Montessori Manipulatives

The Montessori Casa's child-centered holistic form of education strives to bring every child to his fullest potential by providing activities and experiences that support his physical, intellectual, and emotional well-being. Children under the age of six or seven learn best through purposeful, concrete, freely chosen

---

[1] Montessori, Maria. *Dr. Montessori's Own Handbook*. Mineola: Dover Publications, 2005. Print. Pages 10-87.

[2] Montessori, Maria. *The Child, Society and the World: Unpublished Speeches and Writings*. Vol. 7. Oxford: Clio, 2006. Print. The Clio Montessori Ser. Pages 64-67.

[3] Montessori, Maria. *The Advanced Montessori Method I*. Vol. 9. Oxford: Clio, 2004. Print. The Clio Montessori Ser. Pages 98-110.

[4] Montessori, Maria. *Dr. Montessori's Own Handbook*. Mineola: Dover Publications, 2005. Print. Pages 129-136.

activities that engage one or more of the five senses: vision, hearing, smell, touch, and taste.[5] Didactic materials in the Casa that help children learn independently with minimal adult assistance are called "manipulatives." Each scientifically designed and tested manipulative in the Casa is naturally attractive to young children due to the material's hands-on nature that appeals to the senses. In addition to manipulatives, students learn intangible skills such as good manners and strong vocabulary development in a clear, direct manner best suited to their age and level of cognitive development.

Activities and manipulatives in the Casa are divided into four main areas of focus: Practical Life, Sensorial, Language, and Mathematics. Practical Life exercises emphasize life skills that foster hygiene, manners, coordination, personal responsibility, environmental responsibility, and functional independence. Sensorial activities highlight the five senses and their qualities. "Qualities" are the perceptible aspects of a given sense. The visual sense, for instance, has three qualities or three aspects that can be perceived by the human eye: dimension, shape, and color. Students have the opportunity to explore each quality through separate Sensorial manipulatives. Mixed Impressions Sensorial manipulatives, which combine two or more qualities, are introduced following mastery of each quality in isolation. Formal and informal Language exercises foster positive communication skills including diplomacy. Language activities also promote language appreciation, literacy, and creative writing. Mathematics exercises are divided into six categories or groups which cover parallel and sequential skills from basic counting through calculations in the four operations of mathematics (addition, subtraction, multiplication, and division) into the millions. Fractions from one whole through ten-tenths along with simple fraction equations in the four operations of mathematics are also introduced and practiced near the end of a student's stay in the

---

[5] Ibid. Pages 18-87.

Casa. Activities such as art, art appreciation, music, music appreciation, music literacy, botany, geography, history, and science once belonged to a separate subject area known as Cultural Extensions. In the 1990s, the AMI Board wove all Cultural Extensions activities into the other four areas of focus (Practical Life, Sensorial, Language, and Mathematics) to prevent them from being considered superfluous or abandoned in favor of so-called academic subjects. Nothing has been removed from the holistic Montessori Primary curriculum. Only the organization of the Cultural Extensions exercises has changed. Be aware that Montessori teachers before and after the Cultural Extension change may have different organizational styles based upon when they received their training.

When a child in the Casa uses a freely chosen manipulative following an initial presentation from the guide, this is called the child's "work." In Montessori education, "work" does not mean drudgery or obligation; rather, "work" is defined as being fully engaged in a given useful task voluntarily.[6] It is essential that children be given ample opportunity to work with cognitively appropriate, freely chosen materials in order to best serve their developmental needs and interests. To ensure students have adequate time to explore manipulatives independently, a three hour uninterrupted work period is a staunch requirement. During this three hour time block, students are active learners who are at liberty to choose any available material[7] following an initial presentation from the guide.[8]

In the Casa, every child learns at his own pace. To protect each child's natural rate of learning, there are no whole-class

---

[6] Montessori, Maria. *The Absorbent Mind.* Trans. Claude A. Claremont. Vol. 1. Oxford: Clio, 2004. Print. The Clio Montessori Ser. Pages 183-188.

[7] Montessori, Maria. *The Secret of Childhood.* Trans. Barbara B. Carter. Hyderabad: Orient Longman, 2006. Print. Pages 126-127.

[8] Montessori, Maria. *The Discovery of the Child.* Trans. Mary A. Johnstone. Chennai: Kalakshetra, 2006. Print. Pages 87-88.

lessons presented at an arbitrarily determined time throughout the day. Traditional group activities such as the guide reading a story to her class are invitational rather than mandated. If a child is engaged in individual work, the guide will not force him to stop what he is doing to join the group for an adult-imposed "Story Time." Instead, each student is free to continue his work or join the guide's group as he chooses in accordance with the Montessori philosophy of freedom of work choice within natural limits. At any given moment in the Casa, there will be children of the same age with different skill levels working with various materials in different subject areas independently[9] or in small groups.[10] By spending three to four years in the same Casa with the same teacher, a child has plenty of time to learn and explore all the activities in the room before moving on to elementary school at six or seven years of age. This humane pace and respect for the child's individual rate of learning help create a peaceful atmosphere that provides a catalyst for spontaneous pro-social behavior.[11]

Freedom of Movement

In order to make the best use of the official Primary manipulatives, students require freedom of movement and freedom of choice during their uninterrupted three hour work period. "Freedom of movement" means that a child is at liberty to move anywhere in the Casa at will as long as his movements do not impede or interrupt the activities of other students. The ability to move freely throughout the Casa allows students to unobtrusively

---

[9] Ibid.

[10] Montessori, Maria. *The Secret of Childhood*. Trans. Barbara B. Carter. Hyderabad: Orient Longman, 2006. Print. Page 147.

[11] Montessori, Maria. *The Absorbent Mind*. Trans. Claude A. Claremont. Vol. 1. Oxford: Clio, 2004. Print. The Clio Montessori Ser. Pages 183-188.

observe others at work and converse with peers in addition to selecting individual work. Freedom of movement also allows a child to decide where he would like to work. Child-sized tables and rugs are provided to help the student define his workspace and to control clutter. While the child is required to work at either a table or rug for most activities, he may decide where he would like to place a work rug or select any available table where he would like to sit. A student in a Montessori Casa is permitted to move a work table to a more suitable location indoors or outdoors if desired as long as a friend helps him carry the table due to its size and weight. The only other restriction placed upon laying out a work rug or moving a table is that the chosen workspace may not block a shelf containing manipulatives or otherwise obstruct the movements of fellow students.

Once a workspace is established according to the natural rules of the Casa, the child must keep his activities contained within the confines of his chosen work area. Besides providing an effective means of clutter control, a clearly defined workspace promotes respect for personal space. Unless participating in a small group activity, a student may not touch, step on, or otherwise intrude upon another student's workspace without the working child's permission. When a child is finished working with a particular activity, he must put the manipulatives away in their original condition on the shelf. Following cleanup, the child may select new work and bring it to the same workspace or choose a new workspace before selecting a new activity. These rules support the Montessori philosophy of freedom within natural limits, a philosophy that helps create a harmonious environment for everyone.[12]

Freedom of movement extends beyond the indoor Montessori environment into the outdoor classroom. There is generally no set

---

[12] Montessori, Maria. *The Discovery of the Child*. Trans. Mary A. Johnstone. Chennai: Kalakshetra, 2006. Print. Pages 74-80, 85-88.

recess time unless mandated by local law. In Montessori education, the prepared outdoor environment is regarded as a natural extension of the prepared indoor environment, not a break or escape from classwork. Whenever possible, a Montessori Casa provides a fenced outdoor area adjacent to the indoor classroom so that students may safely go outdoors at will without assistance provided they are dressed appropriately for the weather. Experiences such as gardening and botany are both educational fields best learned outdoors. Traditional childhood games like hide and seek, tag, and jump rope promote physical fitness as well as the opportunity to take turns and otherwise get along with one another. On pleasant days, activities from the classroom such as reading, painting, and geography puzzles can be taken to tables that are located outside so that children can enjoy the fresh air while they work.[13] [14] Students may also go outside just to run around to cure a case of the wiggles, a completely normal symptom of childhood.[15]

Above all, freedom of movement fosters functional independence, respects an individual child's interests at a given time, and affirms each student's autonomy, the liberty to act freely within the framework of the Casa. Freedom of movement between the indoor and outdoor classrooms within natural limits allows a child to make spontaneous discoveries about the world around him and helps combat behavior problems and conflicts that stem from an overly restrictive atmosphere.[16] Adherence to the principle of

[13] Montessori, Maria. "The House of Children." *The NAMTA Journal* 38.1 (2013): 11-19. Print.

[14] Montessori, Maria. "Nature in Education." *The NAMTA Journal* 38.1 (2013): 21-27. Print.

[15] Stephenson, Susan. "ADHD and Montessori: A Case Study: Denise's Visit to California April-June, 1996." *The Michael Olaf Montessori Company*. Michael Olaf Montessori Company, 2006. Web. Pages 2-3. 14 Nov. 2014. <http://www.michaelolaf.net/ADHD.pdf>.

[16] Montessori, Maria. *Dr. Montessori's Own Handbook*. Mineola: Dover Publications, 2005. Print. Pages 129-136.

freedom of movement within a high-functioning, well-prepared Montessori environment promotes readiness for internal and external peace.[17] Peace internalized in early childhood in the Primary prepared environment lays a vital foundation for implementing conflict resolution skills in adulthood to solve everyday problems for lasting harmony.[18]

Mixed-age Groups and Class Size

Providing a complete set of Montessori Primary manipulatives for use during an uninterrupted three hour work period is not enough to create an optimal environment for young learners.[19] The provision of developmentally appropriate mixed-age groups of children in each Casa is vital to the Primary prepared environment. A high-functioning Montessori Casa should have a well-balanced proportion of three through six year old children. The provision of a mixed-age group provides a better reflection of society as a whole than the unnatural compartmentalization inherent in single-age settings.[20] Age groups in Montessori education are in alignment with the universal laws of human development, not when a child's birthday happens to be. There are Four Planes of Development recognized by Montessorians that determine how to best organize different age groups of children. The First Plane of Development, early childhood, lasts from birth to about six years of age. The Second Plane, childhood, encompasses approximately

---

[17] Montessori, Maria. *Creative Development in the Child*. Ed. Rukmini Ramachandran. Vol. 1. Chennai: Kalakshetra, 2007. Print. Pages 6, 57-59, 101.
[18] Montessori, Maria. *The Absorbent Mind*. Trans. Claude A. Claremont. Vol. 1. Oxford: Clio, 2004. Print. The Clio Montessori Ser. Pages 202-211.
[19] Montessori, Maria. *The Advanced Montessori Method I*. Vol. 9. Oxford: Clio, 2004. Print. The Clio Montessori Ser. Page 111.
[20] Montessori, Maria. *The Child, Society, and the World: Unpublished Speeches and Writings*. Vol. 7. Oxford: Clio, 2006. Print. The Clio Montessori Ser. Pages 64-69.

ages six through twelve. The Third Plane, adolescence, lasts approximately from ages twelve through eighteen. The Fourth Plane, young adulthood, lasts from about eighteen through twenty-four years of age. Each of the Four Planes of Development can be further divided into two groups. The two divisions of the First Plane are birth through three years of age and three through six years of age. The second half of the First Plane, ages three through six, is the focus of the Montessori Primary Casa. In the prepared environment for three through six year old students, The Peace Table is included in the Casa for children to work out disagreements and arrive at joint amicable solutions.

Since three through six year olds inhabit the same division of the First Plane of Development, it is imperative that they are allowed to interact, work, and explore in the same classroom together. The cognitively appropriate mixed-age group of three through six year old students in the Casa supports optimal individual and social development.[21] Much like the one-room schoolhouses of long ago, young children have the advantage of observing and learning from older peers. Older children in turn naturally learn the virtues of patience, kindness, empathy, understanding, and compassion when helping younger peers which fosters peaceful cohesiveness. Multi-age interaction is an essential lifelong skill, one that cannot be obtained in a single-age classroom.[22]

Class size is just as important as mixed-age groups to foster positive social relations. An ideal Montessori Casa contains a minimum of twenty-five students. A class of forty students with roughly ten children of each age (ten three year olds, ten four year olds, ten five year olds, and ten six year olds) is best for optimal individual and social development.[23] Contrary to popular belief,

---

[21] Ibid. Pages 64-65, 68-69.

[22] Montessori, Maria. *The Absorbent Mind*. Trans. Claude A. Claremont. Vol. 1. Oxford: Clio, 2004. Print. The Clio Montessori Ser. Pages 205-207.

[23] Montessori, Maria. *The Child, Society and the World: Unpublished Speeches*

smaller class sizes do not necessarily provide a superior learning experience versus larger class sizes. Instead, small class sizes can actually make students too dependent upon adult assistance[24] and do not provide the diversity of social experiences inherent in large class sizes where there is freedom of interaction among students of different ages. [25] [26] Small class sizes further limit the diversity of ages by producing an unbalanced proportion of three, four, five, and six year old students. In a class of fewer than ten students, there may be only one five year old and one six year old available to assist younger peers. This arrangement places too much pressure on the two older children in the room. Contrast this example to an ideal class of forty which is likely to contain ten five year olds and ten six year olds. In a class of forty, there will be approximately twenty older children to serve as models, helpers, and peacemakers for their younger peers, a more balanced proportion than would exist in a classroom with too few students. As for concerns about students not receiving enough individual attention in a larger classroom, this is not an issue in a high-functioning prepared Montessori Casa. Montessori education is a system where students become active, independent, self-directed learners who work individually and in small groups following a one-on-one or small group presentation from the trained Montessori guide.[27] Within the Casa's atmosphere of self-directed learning and respect for one another, constant individual attention

---

and Writings. Vol. 7. Oxford: Clio, 2006. Print. The Clio Montessori Ser. Pages 64-65.

[24] Montessori, Maria. *Creative Development in the Child.* Ed. Rukmini Ramachandran. Vol. 1. Chennai: Kalakshetra, 2007. Print. Pages 181-182.

[25] Montessori, Maria. *The Child, Society, and the World: Unpublished Speeches and Writings.* Vol. 7. Oxford: Clio, 2006. Print. The Clio Montessori Ser. Pages 61-69.

[26] Montessori, Maria. *The Absorbent Mind.* Trans. Claude A. Claremont. Vol. 1. Oxford: Clio, 2004. Print. The Clio Montessori Ser. Pages 202-211.

[27] Montessori, Maria. *The Advanced Montessori Method I.* Vol. 9. Oxford: Clio, 2004. Print. The Clio Montessori Ser. Pages 67-68.

is unnecessary and can actually pose a hindrance to spontaneous discovery and the development of functional independence, skills essential for lifelong success. [28] [29]

The Montessori Guide

The third main element of the Montessori Primary prepared environment is the trained Montessori teacher, or guide. The word "guide" refers to a Montessori teacher's main function in the prepared environment as a person who guides children rather than instructing students using traditional methods.[30] In addition to "guide," a Montessori teacher may also be referred to as a "facilitator" or "director/directress." "Facilitator" refers to the guide's role as a facilitator of student learning. The facilitator makes learning easier for the children by presenting age appropriate lessons with hands-on manipulatives in a clear, direct, and precise manner that permits leeway for the child to learn from the material itself and make independent discoveries. "Director" or "directress" is sometimes used to refer to a Montessori teacher because she directs the Casa by showing students how to maintain and use the prepared environment, presents lessons, and keeps manipulatives organized for ease of independent student use. No matter which term a Montessori guide chooses to use, she adheres to the universal expectations of her profession. A Montessori guide is expected to embody certain traits which enable her to guide students most effectively. In addition to knowing how to present every official manipulative in the Casa, the guide must be a keen observer. Observation encompasses the majority of a

---

[28] Ibid. Pages 232-233.

[29] Montessori, Maria. *The Discovery of the Child*. Trans. Mary A. Johnstone. Chennai: Kalakshetra, 2006. Print. Pages 79-83.

[30] Montessori, Maria. *The Secret of Childhood*. Trans. Barbara B. Carter. Hyderabad: Orient Longman, 2006. Print. Pages 144-148.

Montessori guide's work in the Casa.[31] In order to present materials to each student at the developmentally appropriate time, she must observe the child's behavior to gain a better understanding of his cognitive level, experiences, interests, and sensitivities. The guide's training, experience, lesson albums, and observations allow her to create appropriate lesson plans for each student in her class within the framework of the Montessori Method of Primary education. Constant observations of the class and individual students as well as individualized lesson plans based upon those observations in addition to taking notes for record keeping purposes are time-consuming tasks that require great patience and dedication.

In addition to observation and lesson planning, the guide is entrusted to introduce developmentally appropriate manipulatives to individual students or small groups of students during the uninterrupted three hour work period. Individual or small group lessons introduced by the guide are called "presentations." Since children under six or seven years of age are "parallel learners," meaning they are naturally inclined toward individual work rather than collaborative work,[32] most lessons in the Casa are presented to one student at a time at a child-sized work table or rug. The Montessori guide knows when to present each lesson to each individual child based upon her training and observations of the child's previous experiences and cognitive readiness. Following the guide's initial presentation with a given manipulative, the student to whom the lesson was presented may work with the material as long as he chooses and select that material in the future whenever it is available during the uninterrupted three hour work period without seeking permission. After giving her presentation, the guide retreats to observe, allowing the child to work

---

[31] Montessori, Maria. *The Discovery of the Child*. Trans. Mary A. Johnstone. Chennai: Kalakshetra, 2006. Print. Pages 73-74.

[32] Montessori, Maria. *From Childhood to Adolescence*. Vol. 12. Amsterdam: Montessori-Pierson, 2008. Print. The Montessori Ser. Pages 5-7.

independently or put the manipulative away in its original condition in its proper place to choose other work. Through hands-on work with the manipulatives in the Casa, children become independent, self-directed learners who take turns and respect others' personal space, which in turn helps promote a peaceful environment.

Montessori's child-centered method of education requires the guide to constantly exercise humility. As the name implies, the Children's House, or Casa, is designed for the children rather than the adult. The guide is merely a facilitator for the children's learning. As a Montessori guide's students' independence blossoms, her role becomes increasingly passive while her students become increasingly active. Eventually, a guide should only need to intervene when presenting a new lesson or during an emergency. The guide's goal is for her students to eventually become so independent that they will no longer need her guidance.[33] Once a child has graduated from the Montessori Primary prepared environment, he should be equipped with a foundation in individual, social, academic, and peaceful conflict resolution skills necessary for lifelong success at home, school, and in the wider world. It is only with the solid foundation provided by a carefully prepared environment complete with the entire array of didactic manipulatives, cognitively appropriate mixed-age groups, and the trained guide that a child can truly blossom and eventually transform the world around him for the betterment of humanity.[34]

Daily Rhythm of the Casa

Beginning on the first day of school, students are immersed in

---

[33] Montessori, Maria. *The Absorbent Mind*. Trans. Claude A. Claremont. Vol. 1. Oxford: Clio, 2004. Print. The Clio Montessori Ser. Page 259.
[34] Montessori, Maria. *The Secret of Childhood*. Trans. Barbara B. Carter. Hyderabad: Orient Longman, 2006. Print. Pages 144-151.

the pro-social atmosphere of the Primary prepared environment that constantly exhibits mutual respect between adults and students. This culture of mutual respect begins with the adults in the environment. Every morning before the children arrive, the guide and her assistant ensure the room is prepared for the day. Preparation involves making sure the room and materials are clean and orderly. All manipulatives must be in their correct places on the open shelving, ready for independent student use. A properly prepared Casa demonstrates respect for the students who will be using the room and its materials during school hours, an essential prerequisite for positive teacher-student relationships. Once the room is in order, the guide positions herself near the classroom door in such a manner that will allow her to greet each student individually by name when he enters the Casa. When the first student arrives, the guide crouches so she and the child face each other at eye level. Making eye contact, the guide says, "Good morning, (Name)," as she shakes the child's hand. A new student who is unaccustomed to being greeted in this manner may not yet make eye contact or feel ready to make a reply. The guide makes no issue of a shy or otherwise non-verbal student. Following her greeting, the guide invites the child to hang up his coat, put away his lunchbox, and find some work. Once the child departs, the guide greets the next student. Eventually, with enough repetition of the daily greeting, each child in the Casa should verbally return the guide's salutation. While the nature of the daily greeting varies according to cultural norms, its inclusion in the Montessori Casa is a universal concept. Regardless of whether a daily greeting involves a handshake, a bow, or other cultural gesture, it is essential that each child in the Casa is individually acknowledged by the guide at the beginning of each school day to establish and maintain mutual rapport between the adults and the students in the prepared environment. By greeting each child by name individually, students internalize respect for themselves and others, an important first step to establishing lasting peace in the Casa and wider world.[35]

After a child is greeted individually by the guide, he puts his coat and lunchbox away in their designated locations in the room if applicable. Starting on the first day of school, even the youngest students begin to practice functional independence by hanging up their own coats. If a child comes to class unable to hang up his own coat, he is assisted by the aide or preferably by an older, more experienced student. Often the simple act of placing a coat on a hanger may take a young student a considerable length of time. Since the uninterrupted three hour work period begins immediately following the individual morning greeting, the child can practice hanging up his coat at his own pace. If an older peer provides assistance instead of the aide, both the young child and his older classmate derive positive, lasting social benefits from the experience. By helping a younger peer, the older child naturally exercises positive traits including patience, empathy, and compassion. The younger child in turn has the opportunity to see his older peer as a source of help and companionship rather than a competitor. Peer-to-peer assistance with simple tasks such as hanging up a coat is only the beginning of pro-social, mixed-age interactions in the Casa that foster peaceful problem solving skills throughout the year.[36]

The Three Part Work Cycle

As soon as a child hangs up his coat and puts away his lunchbox following the morning greeting, he is at liberty to choose any available material in the Casa in which he has previously received an initial presentation from the guide. The process of taking a manipulative from the shelf, working with the

---

[35] Ibid. Pages 132-135, 137.

[36] Montessori, Maria. *The Absorbent Mind*. Trans. Claude A. Claremont. Vol. 1. Oxford: Clio, 2004. Print. The Clio Montessori Ser. Pages 205-211.

manipulative, and then returning the manipulative to its proper place on the shelf in its original condition is known as the "Three Part Work Cycle." The Three Part Work Cycle establishes the three main rules in the Casa without resorting to lectures about classroom expectations. Since young children do not respond well to a litany of classroom rules established on the first day of school[37] or criticisms of misbehavior following an infraction,[38] the conditions of the Three Part Work Cycle within the prepared environment provide a framework for proper behavior in the Casa to help prevent conflict.[39]

The Three Part Work Cycle: Part 1

The first part of the Three Part Work Cycle states that any child who has had a lesson in a material may choose that material any time it is available during the three hour uninterrupted work period. This portion of the Three Part Work Cycle establishes and enforces several rules without having to resort to traditional means of conveying classroom policies. "Any child who has had a lesson" means that a child may choose a material only if he has received an initial presentation from the guide. A child who has not had a lesson may not use a material until he receives an official presentation from the guide. In the event that a student takes an unfamiliar material from the shelf, the guide intervenes by saying something like, "Oh, you haven't had a lesson in that material yet. Let's find something you've had a lesson in." The guide may then assist the child in finding familiar work. If a child continues to seek out unfamiliar materials, the guide may show him how to dust a manipulative of interest. By allowing a child to dust an

---

[37] Ibid. Pages 6-7, 190-191.
[38] Ibid. Pages 209-211.
[39] Montessori, Maria. *Creative Development in the Child*. Ed. Rukmini Ramachandran. Vol. 1. Chennai: Kalakshetra, 2007. Print. Pages 163-164.

unfamiliar material, the guide gives the student a purposeful task pertaining to coordination and care of the environment that also satisfies his curiosity about the advanced manipulative. Purposeful interaction with a material also promotes a positive attitude toward learning how to use it in the future when ready. Far from being a restrictive policy, the rule that a child must receive a lesson before working with a material is a measure rooted in safety and common sense. There are many activities in the Casa which are not appropriate for new three year old students due to safety concerns such as "Sewing a Button" which involves the use of a sharp needle. To help prevent accidents, a guide will not present a material that could be hazardous to a child due to his lack of fine motor coordination. The guide presents lessons when she observes that the child is ready to use the activity safely. Another reason why children may not use a material before receiving a lesson is due to the sequential nature of the manipulatives. Most activities in the Casa are designed to build upon skills mastered through previously introduced manipulatives. Any work involving multiplication, for example, cannot be presented before a child masters addition. This is a reasonable policy since multiplication, the addition of like quantities a given number of times, is an extension of previously learned addition skills. To introduce multiplication to a student before he masters addition would be irrational and cause the child unnecessary frustration. The same principle applies to activities in other subject areas such as Practical Life. It stands to reason that a child must learn how button and unbutton buttons before learning how to tie and untie a bow as bow trying requires greater fine motor control and a longer sequence of actions than buttoning. By presenting materials in the correct order, and preventing a student from selecting a material far beyond his cognitive level and skill set, the guide helps prevent frustration and other obstacles to joyful, successful learning. Creating just the right amount of challenge for a child through sequentially organized manipulatives helps keep the child interested in learning as its own reward throughout his stay in the Casa. Without joyful learning experiences, internal peace, the prerequisite to external peace, cannot be achieved.[40]

The stipulation that a child may choose any available material during the uninterrupted three hour work period helps prevent conflict as this rule clearly establishes when a material may be used. "Any available material" means that the material is on the shelf where any child who has received an initial presentation may take it when desired. If a material is not on the shelf, which usually means another child is using it, that material is not available. When a material is not available, the child who wants to use the unavailable material must wait until it becomes available again before using it. Having to wait for a material to become available naturally exercises the child's patience and problem solving skills.[41] The child may sit and wait for the manipulative to become available, or he may select a different activity while waiting. He may also unobtrusively observe a classmate who is working with the desired manipulative. How a student decides to use his time while waiting for a desired activity to become available is a decision the child must make independently. The student may not, however, take the material from another child as this violates the rule that a child may choose "any *available* material." In accordance with this policy, no adult in the room may insist that the child who is using the manipulative share the manipulative or otherwise force him to relinquish it. Since children under the age of six or seven are "parallel learners," meaning they generally prefer to work beside other children rather than with them, the guide respects her students' independent activities. When the child who is working with the manipulative is finished, he must return it to the shelf in its original condition.

---

[40] Ibid. Pages 152-153.
[41] Montessori, Maria. *The Absorbent Mind.* Vol. 1. Oxford: Clio, 2004. Print. The Clio Montessori Ser. Pages 203-204.

Once the material is returned to the shelf in its original condition, any child who has had a lesson in that material may take it. This is a more natural way for young children to share and helps prevent unnecessary conflicts and resentment that could arise from forced sharing.[42] Collaborative learning, or working with peers, is a natural developmental stage that occurs in the Second Plane of Development, typically after a child has surpassed six years of age.[43] Before effective collaboration in older children can occur, the young child's parallel learner stage must be respected so that he may independently develop the life skills necessary for future personal, social, and academic success.[44]

To further aid peaceful conflict resolution skills and to promote respect for the materials, generally only one of each manipulative is provided in the Casa. Having only one of each material in the Casa promotes patience and careful handling of objects. With only one of each activity in the room, children learn that they must wait their turn to use a currently unavailable activity, further fostering patience and problem solving skills. Whenever possible, manipulatives are made from natural materials such as wood, metal, glass, and ceramics rather than plastic for aesthetics and to promote careful use. The prevalence of finite, high-quality, natural materials in the Casa helps children realize they must be careful when using an object in the room because there are no immediate replacements for it.[45] If something breaks, safe clean-up practices are observed. The teacher or assistant carefully supervises and assists any child who is sweeping up a broken material. After the broken pieces are disposed of, life in the

---

[42] Montessori, Maria. *Creative Development in the Child*. Ed. Rukmini Ramachandran. Vol. 1. Chennai: Kalakshetra, 2007. Print. Pages 163-164.

[43] Montessori, Maria. *To Educate the Human Potential*. Vol. 6. Oxford: Clio, 2003. Print. The Clio Montessori Ser. Pages 3-4.

[44] Ibid. Pages 3-5.

[45] Montessori, Maria. *The Child, Society, and the World*. Vol. 7. Oxford: Clio, 2006. Print. The Clio Montessori Ser. Page 64.

Casa continues as usual. No child is ever shamed for breaking an object. Instead, the teacher or assistant may demonstrate at a later time how to carry a given object in a way that it is less likely to fall and break. If the broken or damaged object is part of set of manipulatives, the entire material must be put away until a replacement can be found. Putting the entire material away is not a punishment but a natural consequence. A Hand Washing activity station with a broken soap dish, for example, must be put away until a new soap dish is found to help preserve the accuracy of the activity. An activity with missing parts in not acceptable in a Montessori Casa as it gives students an inaccurate impression of how the material is supposed to function. Leaving materials in disrepair is also disrespectful to the students who have a reasonable expectation that all manipulatives in the Casa are complete, accurate, and ready for them to use. Once a replacement is found, the material is returned to the Casa. The reintroduction of a repaired material to the Casa may subconsciously encourage students to handle the manipulative with greater care in the future to help keep it in the room for everyone to enjoy. Careful handling promoted by the scarcity and delicacy of the objects in the environment is an important lifelong skill that must be internalized in order for peace and responsibility to emerge.[46] Like the manipulatives in the Casa, many resources in the wider world are scarce and therefore must be treated with care. This is a lesson that must be illustrated concretely with the tangible, breakable, finite manipulatives in the Primary prepared environment as a young child typically cannot act upon the abstract verbal admonition, "Be careful with that!"[47] It is through the fragile materials in the environment and modeling of their proper use that gentleness can

---

[46] Montessori, Maria. *The Advanced Montessori Method I*. Vol. 9. Oxford: Clio, 2004. Print. The Clio Montessori Ser. Pages 231-233.

[47] Montessori, Maria. *The Absorbent Mind*. Trans. Claude A. Claremont. Vol. 1. Oxford: Clio, 2004. Print. The Clio Montessori Ser. Pages 190-191, 219-220, 224.

be internalized effectively and applied to the world outside the Casa.[48]

In addition to establishing rules for the children, the first part of the Three Part Work Cycle enforces adult behavior in the Casa. When a child chooses an available material in which he has received an initial presentation, the guide respects his work choice. In an authentic Montessori prepared environment, this means that the guide may not insist the child choose a different material on the grounds that he has worked with a given manipulative several times before. Acting upon societal demands for increased emphasis on academics, some Montessori Casas implement a policy of requiring older Primary children to only choose academic materials during work time, typically manipulatives from Language and Mathematics. Other Casas demand that students choose at least one academic material during the afternoon work period before selecting any Practical Life exercises. These policies are in direct violation of the Montessori tenet of student freedom of work choice when selecting materials. In accordance with the first part of the Three Part Work Cycle, *any* available material may be chosen by any child who has had a lesson in that material. This means that if a child wishes to work only with Practical Life activities on a given day, that is his choice and his choice alone. To require a child to choose an "academic material" before he may do further Practical Life work is in opposition to Montessori pedagogy.[49] Also, by prohibiting students from using Practical Life materials before completing a so-called "intellectual activity," children may receive the subconscious message that intellectual work is superior to manual work. Such a policy may therefore induce subconscious prejudices in students about adults who work

---

[48] Montessori, Maria. *The Advanced Montessori Method I*. Vol. 9. Oxford: Clio, 2004. Print. The Clio Montessori Ser. Pages 231-233.

[49] Montessori, Maria. "Some Words of Advice to Teachers, 1924." *The Call of Education* 11.IV (1925). *Montessori Article*. Association Montessori Internationale, 2005. Web. 3 Jun. 2011.

with their hands such as tradesmen. Subconscious prejudices induced by misapplication of the first part of the Three Part Work Cycle can be an obstacle to understanding and respecting the work of others as well as undermine peaceful human relations.

The Three Part Work Cycle: Part II

The second part of the Three Part Work Cycle states that the child may work with the material he has chosen for as long as he wants during the uninterrupted work period. This rule implies that the child is using the material for its intended purpose. While spontaneous discoveries with the manipulatives, known as variations, are encouraged, misusing materials is prohibited.[50] An example of material misuse is if a child uses the shortest Red Rod, a manipulative designed for the exploration of length, as a drumstick, which could damage the material. In this situation, the guide may intervene and tell the child to put the material away and take out the musical instruments since it is obvious that the child is not currently interested in exploring one-dimensional change. The guide is careful during any intervention to not discourage or otherwise upset the child. To protect the material and help the child choose more appropriate work that is in alignment with his current interest and level of energy, the guide may say, "It's time to put away the Red Rods and take out the drum!" By remaining upbeat during an intervention, the guide manages to encourage the child to explore his current interest through a constructive outlet without thwarting him. In doing so, the guide maintains Montessori's philosophy of joyful learning within natural limits as a precursor to personal, social, and academic success throughout childhood and into adulthood.

A child who is working with a manipulative properly at an

---

[50] Montessori, Maria. *The Discovery of the Child*. Trans. Mary A. Johnstone. Chennai: Kalakshetra, 2006. Print. Pages 184-186.

appropriate workspace such as a child-sized table or rug may continue to work as long as he pleases during the uninterrupted work period. This means that a child who is working may not be interrupted by other students or adults in the Casa. If a child disturbs a classmate who is working, the guide distracts the interrupting student with an interesting activity.[51] To emphasize that the student working with a manipulative is busy, the guide may say to the interrupting child, "(Name) is doing work now. He is not available for a conversation." Depending upon the individual child and the circumstances, the guide may then invite the child to choose individual work or attend a small group activity. If the child is in a particularly talkative mood, the guide may help him find a student who is available to have a conversation at the Conversation Bench, a place in the Casa where children can converse freely to help develop positive language and communication skills. Alternatively, she may lead him in an adult-directed "Facilitated Conversation" to strengthen the child's language abilities and foster the art of conversation. Learning how to determine whether or not someone is "available" for a conversation or a small group activity is an essential skill that begins on the first day of school. Understanding "available" and "not available" enforces respect for the work of others and sets clear limits about personal space. Not only does a child in the Casa learn not to disturb a classmate at work, he also learns how to set limits with his words using positive phrasing if he is interrupted by another student while working. If a working child is disturbed by a classmate, he should say, "I'm not available for a conversation. I'm doing work now." Toward students who are encroaching upon his workspace or crowding him, a working child can say, "You can take a step away from my work." These early experiences of setting limits through positive phrasing are the first

---

[51] Montessori, Maria. *The Absorbent Mind.* Vol. 1. Oxford: Clio, 2004. Print. The Clio Montessori Ser. Pages 254-255.

steps toward future diplomacy and negotiation.

In addition to protecting working students from peer interruptions, the second part of the Three Part Work Cycle also enforces boundaries with the adults in the room. Just as a child may not disturb a fellow student's work, neither may the guide nor her assistant.[52] The adult may only interrupt a student's work if he is posing a danger to himself or others, being disruptive toward others, misusing a material, needs a specific point of interest to ensure proper material use, during transition times such as lunch and pick-up time, or during an emergency. Beyond these safety measures, the guide and her assistant are bound to the same rules as the students when it comes to respecting work. If a guide would like to present a lesson to an individual student, she must wait for that student to become available before approaching him. By adhering to the same rule about not interrupting work as her students, the guide demonstrates that respect for work and personal space are universal expectations regardless of age and status. Refraining from interfering in the child's work also allows concentration to develop, an essential prerequisite to success in the Casa and wider world.[53] When everyone follows the universal rules of the prepared environment, strong rapport and harmony develop to create the peaceful, pro-social culture of the Casa[54] that lays a foundation for peace outside the classroom.[55]

Besides establishing universal expectations, not permitting a working student to be disturbed during the uninterrupted three hour work period creates a safe and relaxed environment where joyful learning as its own reward as well as concentration can flourish. If children were constantly interrupted or herded around in groups,

---

[52] Ibid. Pages 255-256.

[53] Ibid.

[54] Montessori, Maria. *Creative Development in the Child.* Ed. Rukmini Ramachandran. Vol. 1. Chennai: Kalakshetra, 2007. Print. Pages 163-164.

[55] Montessori, Maria. *The Absorbent Mind.* Trans. Claude A. Claremont. Vol. 1. Oxford: Clio, 2004. Print. The Clio Montessori Ser. Pages 183-190, 202-212.

there would be little time for independent discoveries. The provision of a three hour work period, in which a student may work with any previously presented material for as long as he desires, allows the child to learn at his own pace without feeling rushed. When working at the humane, leisurely pace provided by the open-ended uninterrupted time block with freedom of work choice, students have the opportunity to focus upon topics of interest without worrying about artificial demarcations of time punctuated by blaring school bells. Removing the stress that comes from assigned work to be completed during inadequate periods of time helps students cultivate a positive attitude toward lifelong learning and fosters pro-social human relationships. This positive attitude toward learning created by the prepared environment fosters spontaneous concentration that helps students acquire internal peace, a vital prerequisite to positive social relations and external peace.[56]

The Three Part Work Cycle: Part III

The third part of the Three Part Work Cycle states that a child must return the material to its proper place in its original condition when finished working, at which point any child who has had a lesson in that material may choose the material. Returning a material to its proper place in the Casa in its original condition fosters order, responsibility, and respect for both the materials and fellow students. "In its original condition" means that the material is clean, orderly, and ready for the next child to use. Ideally, the material should look as though it were not used at all. While all children in the Casa are expected to clean up after themselves in this manner to foster cleanliness, responsibility, strong work ethic, and functional independence, it is important to note that a young

---

[56] Ibid.

student who has just learned how to use a material may not be able to return the manipulative to the shelf in its original condition due to lack of experience. In this case, the child is still expected to clean up after himself and put the manipulative away to the best of his ability. A child who has just learned how to use the Shoelace Frame, for example, may not yet be able to tie a bow. Following the third part of the Three Part Work Cycle for this inexperienced student may mean that he returns the Shoelace Frame to its correct shelf or basket but with the bow untied. Alternatively, the child may ask an older student to tie the bow for him before he returns the material to the shelf. For a young learner, this is sufficient until he perfects his fine motor coordination skills to the point where he can tie a bow independently.

If a manipulative is not returned properly due to a young child's lack of experience, neither the guide nor the aide corrects the child or fixes the material. It is essential that an adult in a Montessori Casa never cleans or tidies the room while students are present as this gives children the false impression that the adults in the Casa exist to clean up after them. The exception to this policy is if the adult eats lunch with the children, in which case, the adult cleans up after herself to model personal responsibility. But to put away materials on a student's behalf is in violation of the third part of the Three Part Work Cycle which dictates that the *child* who is finished using a material must return it to its proper place in the Casa in its original condition. In the event that a manipulative is not put away correctly by a younger child who lacks experience, an older child who is unsettled by the lack of order presented by a material in disarray is free to assist his younger peer by putting the material away properly, which fosters social cohesion.[57] [58] It is important to note that no child is forced to clean up after another.[59]

---

[57] Montessori, Maria. *Creative Development in the Child.* Ed. Rukmini Ramachandran. Vol. 1. Chennai: Kalakshetra, 2007. Print. Pages 69-70.
[58] Montessori, Maria. *The Absorbent Mind.* Trans. Claude A. Claremont. Vol. 1. Oxford: Clio, 2004. Print. The Clio Montessori Ser. Pages 206-207, 212-213.

Rather, an older child preparing a material that is in disarray does so spontaneously out of a desire to help his younger peers and to make the room look nice for his fellow students.[60] If the material is not fixed by an older child by the end of the school day, the adult prepares the material for the following school day after the children have left the classroom.

While a younger child may have difficulty putting materials away properly due to lack of experience or coordination skills, a child is not allowed to put manipulatives away in a disorderly fashion if the guide knows the student is capable of putting the material away in its original condition. If a capable child fails to put a material away properly, the guide intervenes immediately by saying something like, "Let's make sure this material is ready for the next person to use." The guide gives additional prompts as necessary while the child prepares the material. Only after the capable student has put the material away in its original condition, which shows respect for his fellow classmates, may he select a new activity.[61]

Intrinsic Rewards and Control of Error

The rhythm of the Three Part Work Cycle (choosing work, using work, and putting work away in its original condition) provides the necessary framework in the prepared environment for effective freedom of choice within natural limits. When students choose cognitively appropriate activities that align with their current interests, they acquire the virtues of self-esteem and learning as its own reward. Joyful spontaneous learning in the

---

[59] Ibid. Pages 206-207.

[60] Montessori, Maria. *Dr. Montessori's Own Handbook*. Mineola: Dover Publications, 2005. Print. Pages 25-27.

[61] Montessori, Maria. *Creative Development in the Child*. Ed. Rukmini Ramachandran. Vol. 1. Chennai: Kalakshetra, 2007. Print. Pages 163-164.

Casa is possible because the prepared environment does not use rewards or punishments to support skill acquisition. Children are neither rewarded nor punished for their work in the Casa because it would be detrimental to their learning.[62] If children were given gold stars for their work[63] or forced to work under the threat of punishment, they would be unlikely to ever learn for the sake of learning.[64] [65] The reward children receive from their work is the intrinsic satisfaction they gain from their accomplishments.[66] [67]

Just as detrimental to a positive learning experience as gold stars and bad marks on a paper are praise and criticism. Rather than learning directly from the guide and seeking her approval and correction, students learn from the materials themselves following an initial presentation[68] that clearly demonstrates how the manipulative is used in the most straightforward manner possible.[69] Following the initial presentation, the teacher withdraws and allows the manipulative to become the child's guide to independent learning. The presented manipulative then acts as an

---

[62] Montessori, Maria. *The Absorbent Mind*. Trans. Claude A. Claremont. Vol. 1. Oxford: Clio, 2004. Print. The Clio Montessori Ser. Pages 223-229.

[63] Kohn, Alfie. *Punished by Rewards: The Trouble with Gold Stars, Incentive Plans, A's, Praise, and Other Bribes*. New York: Houghton Mifflin, 1993. Print. Page 17.

[64] Montessori, Maria. *Creative Development in the Child*. Ed. Rukmini Ramachandran. Vol. 1. Chennai: Kalakshetra, 2007. Print. Pages 152-153.

[65] Kohn, Alfie. *Punished by Rewards: The Trouble with Gold Stars, Incentive Plans, A's, Praise, and Other Bribes*. New York: Houghton Mifflin, 1993. Print. Page 105.

[66] Montessori, Maria. *The Secret of Childhood*. Trans. Barbara B. Carter. Hyderabad: Orient Longman, 2006. Print. Pages 131-132.

[67] Kohn, Alfie. *Punished by Rewards: The Trouble with Gold Stars, Incentive Plans, A's, Praise, and Other Bribes*. New York: Houghton Mifflin, 1993. Print. Pages 96-116.

[68] Montessori, Maria. *The Advanced Montessori Method I*. Vol. 9. Oxford: Clio, 2004. Print. The Clio Montessori Ser. Pages 67-68.

[69] Montessori, Maria. *The Discovery of the Child*. Trans. Mary A. Johnstone. Chennai: Kalakshetra, 2006. Print. Pages 184, 186-194.

unbiased teacher that provides immediate feedback for student performance. The self-correcting nature of the manipulative, known as the "control of error,"[70] eliminates the need for most external interference from the guide.[71] For example, in the Cylinder Blocks, an early Sensorial manipulative that allows a student to explore three-dimensional spatial relationships by taking cylinders in and out of their corresponding holes in a wooden block, each cylinder corresponds to only one correct hole. If a child places a cylinder in an incorrect hole, there is no need for the guide to tell the child he is wrong or give him a red mark on a paper. Instead, the material itself tells the child he has made a mistake because it is visually obvious that the cylinder does not fit in the chosen hole correctly. Without any prompting from an external source other than the manipulative, the child should remove the cylinder and place it into a different hole until he finds the correct one. When finished, all cylinders should be in their correct holes. This experience of individual accomplishment is rewarding enough to encourage repeat use of the manipulative.[72] No praise or gold stars are necessary for the child to complete the task as the manipulative is naturally appealing to the child's sensitive periods for order, movement, and refinement of sensory perception. Often called "windows of opportunity" or "critical periods" in non-Montessori education courses, "sensitive periods" are intense motivations for the acquisition of order, movement, refinement of sensory perception, and language in First Plane children. The sensitive periods for order, movement, and refinement of sensory perception begin to fade[73] when a child is

---

[70] Montessori, Maria. *The Absorbent Mind*. Trans. Claude A. Claremont. Vol. 1. Oxford: Clio, 2004. Print. The Clio Montessori Ser. Page 226.

[71] Montessori, Maria. *Creative Development in the Child*. Ed. Rukmini Ramachandran. Vol. 1. Chennai: Kalakshetra, 2007. Print. Pages 58, 139-140.

[72] Montessori, Maria. *The Absorbent Mind*. Trans. Claude A. Claremont. Vol. 1. Oxford: Clio, 2004. Print. The Clio Montessori Ser. Pages 227-228.

[73] Montessori, Maria. *Creative Development in the Child*. Ed. Rukmini

about four-and-a-half years of age.[74] Language remains an intense motivation through the age of six.[75] By appealing to the child's sensitive periods at the developmentally appropriate time rather than using rewards and punishments, the Montessori Casa's prepared environment is ideal for fostering lifelong learning as its own reward.

While praise is not issued as a reward in the Casa due to its inherent obstacle to learning,[76] there are times when a student may want to share his joy in completing a task with the guide or her assistant. When a child wants to show an adult in the room his work, he is free to ask her to look at it as long as she is available. If the guide or aide is available, she gladly accompanies the child to his workspace at his request.[77] The adult respectfully looks at the child's completed work without touching it and says something like, "Thank you for letting me admire your work." Usually this neutral response is enough to satisfy a child's emotional need to share his accomplishments with others. If a child asks for the guide or aide's opinion, she is careful to acknowledge the child's accomplishment without resorting to direct praise or advice. Instead of conveying verbal approval, the adult emphasizes in simple language how the child should take pride in his own work without seeking the approbation of others. Usually, the adult expresses this sentiment by saying, "I can see you worked really hard on that. You must be so proud of yourself!" The adult then excuses herself to perform other tasks which require her attention. When the adult in the Casa deflects praise by turning the feeling of accomplishment back over to the student, she helps foster the

---

Ramachandran. Vol. 1. Chennai: Kalakshetra, 2007. Print. Pages 17-25.

[74] Montessori, Maria. *The Discovery of the Child*. Trans. Mary A. Johnstone. Chennai: Kalakshetra, 2006. Print. Pages 244-245.

[75] Ibid. Page 292.

[76] Montessori, Maria. *The Absorbent Mind*. Vol. 1. Oxford: Clio, 2004. Print. The Clio Montessori Ser. Page 255.

[77] Ibid. Page 256.

intrinsic nature of personal pride in work well done. Having pride in one's own accomplishments rather than seeking the external validation of others helps foster confidence, self-esteem, and self-motivation, all essential attributes for fostering intellectual and emotional growth as well as developing positive social relations.[78]

Normalization

The intrinsic rewards and self-motivation that come from working with developmentally appropriate, hands-on, freely chosen activities in the Primary prepared environment lay a vital foundation for concentration which in turn fosters "normalization." Normalization is the process in which a student spontaneously and effortlessly abandons all negative behaviors in exchange for positive behaviors.[79] The behaviors of a normalized child include kindness, patience, helpfulness, empathy, [80] hospitality,[81] pride in one's individual accomplishments, joy for the success of others,[82] inner discipline,[83] self-regulation, self-confidence,[84] voluntary rejection of external rewards,[85] and the ability to choose activities and concentrate upon them without adult interference or guidance.[86]

---

[78] Kohn, Alfie. *Punished by Rewards: The Trouble with Gold Stars, Incentive Plans, A's, Praise, and Other Bribes*. New York: Houghton Mifflin, 1993. Print. Pages 54-59, 96-116.

[79] Montessori, Maria. *The Absorbent Mind*. Vol. 1. Oxford: Clio, 2004. Print. The Clio Montessori Ser. Pages 183-188, 190.

[80] Ibid. Pages 183-188.

[81] Montessori, Maria. *The Secret of Childhood*. Trans. Barbara B. Carter. Hyderabad: Orient Longman, 2006. Print. Pages 133-135, 137.

[82] Montessori, Maria. *The Absorbent Mind*. Vol. 1. Oxford: Clio, 2004. Print. The Clio Montessori Ser. Pages 210-211, 220.

[83] Ibid. Pages 183-184.

[84] Montessori, Maria. *The Secret of Childhood*. Trans. Barbara B. Carter. Hyderabad: Orient Longman, 2006. Print. Pages 177-178.

[85] Ibid. Pages 128-129.

[86] Ibid. Pages 92-94.

A child who is not yet normalized is considered "collective stage." Children in the collective stage exhibit abnormal behaviors known as "deviations." These deviations vary by child and include diverse negative traits ranging from aggression to timidity. All deviations, regardless of type, disappear instantly upon the onset of normalization in young children, at which point the aforementioned positive traits are spontaneously adopted.[87] Normalization is a universal phenomenon that has been observed in young children for more than one hundred years on every inhabited continent within every social class.[88] It is traditionally believed that only children under the age of six or seven are capable of achieving normalization,[89] although exceptions may exist.[90] True internal and external peace can emerge only after normalization has been awakened.[91]

A Montessori guide's most important goal is to ensure that every student in her class achieves normalization[92] before leaving the Casa to attend elementary school. Normalization, the process in which a child spontaneously abandons all negative behaviors in exchange for positive behaviors, is both the result of and the prerequisite to a young child's education in the Casa.[93] It is only after an individual student is normalized that joyful academic achievement[94] [95] and true harmony are possible.[96] Before a child is

---

[87] Montessori, Maria. *The Absorbent Mind.* Vol. 1. Oxford: Clio, 2004. Print. The Clio Montessori Ser. Pages 183-186.

[88] Ibid. Page 185.

[89] Montessori, Maria. *Creative Development in the Child.* Ed. Rukmini Ramachandran. Vol. 1. Chennai: Kalakshetra, 2007. Print. Pages 233-234.

[90] Montessori, Maria. *The Secret of Childhood.* Trans. Barbara B. Carter. Hyderabad: Orient Longman, 2006. Print. Page 158.

[91] Montessori, Maria. *The Absorbent Mind.* Vol. 1. Oxford: Clio, 2004. Print. The Clio Montessori Ser. Pages 212-222.

[92] Ibid. Page 186.

[93] Ibid. Page 188.

[94] Montessori, Maria. *Dr. Montessori's Own Handbook.* Mineola: Dover Publications, 2005. Print. Pages 91-94.

normalized, the guide prepares the environment to allow normalization to occur. As an internal quality, normalization cannot be artificially induced or forced.[97] Normalization is instead acquired through concentration upon freely chosen, age-appropriate manipulatives that appeal to a young child's sensitive periods. In general, normalization emerges through voluntary, repeated use of Practical Life manipulatives,[98] although some students may acquire normalization through Sensorial activities or art.[99] Normalization through hands-on academic materials such as those found in Mathematics is rare but possible in certain cases.[100] In general, it is the Practical Life and Sensorial manipulatives which internally drive children to exercise their sensitive periods for order, movement, and the refinement of sensory perception, all of which naturally encourage repetition.[101] It is normal and not uncommon for a young child to repeat an exercise forty to fifty times in succession[102] to perfect newfound skills[103] and satisfy an internal emotional need.[104] The spontaneous repetition of hands-

---

[95] Montessori, Maria. *The Child, Society, and the World: Unpublished Speeches and Writings*. Vol. 7. Oxford: Clio, 2006. Print. The Clio Montessori Ser. Pages 21-22.

[96] Montessori, Maria. *The Absorbent Mind*. Vol. 1. Oxford: Clio, 2004. Print. The Clio Montessori Ser. Pages 212-222.

[97] Ibid. Page 185.

[98] Montessori, Maria. *Creative Development in the Child*. Ed. Rukmini Ramachandran. Vol. 1. Chennai: Kalakshetra, 2007. Print. Pages 52-59, 95, 182-183.

[99] Montessori, Maria. *The Advanced Montessori Method I*. Vol. 9. Oxford: Clio, 2004. Print. The Clio Montessori Ser. Pages 70-75.

[100] Montessori, Maria. *The Secret of Childhood*. Trans. Barbara B. Carter. Hyderabad: Orient Longman, 2006. Print. Pages 153-154.

[101] Montessori, Maria. *Creative Development in the Child*. Ed. Rukmini Ramachandran. Vol. 1. Chennai: Kalakshetra, 2007. Print. Pages 52-63, 89-101.

[102] Montessori, Maria. *The Secret of Childhood*. Trans. Barbara B. Carter. Hyderabad: Orient Longman, 2006. Print. Pages 124-126.

[103] Montessori, Maria. *Dr. Montessori's Own Handbook*. Mineola: Dover Publications, 2005. Print. Pages 21-21.

on, developmentally appropriate exercises leads to concentration, an essential prerequisite to normalization.[105] Since most children first achieve concentration followed by normalization through Practical Life exercises, Practical Life is the starting point for every child's education in the Casa.[106] Practical Life exercises such as hand washing, dusting, sweeping, baking, shoe polishing, and shoe tying improve skills related to hygiene[107] as well as gross and fine motor skills.[108]

Exactly when normalization occurs depends upon the individual child. Normalization of the individual child can take anywhere from a few days to a year.[109] Factors that may inhibit the awakening of normalization may include an improperly prepared environment, the child's age, or disabilities.[110] The sensitive periods for order, movement, refinement of sensory perception, and language, which strongly motivate a child to seek out certain experiences in his environment for his holistic development,[111] are most intense when a child is under four-and-a-half years of age.[112] As young as he is, a new five year old in a Montessori Casa may not arrive at normalization as easily as his

---

[104] Montessori, Maria. *The Secret of Childhood.* Trans. Barbara B. Carter. Hyderabad: Orient Longman, 2006. Print. Pages 125-126.

[105] Montessori, Maria. *The Absorbent Mind.* Vol. 1. Oxford: Clio, 2004. Print. The Clio Montessori Ser. Page 188.

[106] Montessori, Maria. *The Secret of Childhood.* Trans. Barbara B. Carter. Hyderabad: Orient Longman, 2006. Print. Pages 82-86.

[107] Ibid. Ibid. Pages 125-126.

[108] Montessori, Maria. *Dr. Montessori's Own Handbook.* Mineola: Dover Publications, 2005. Print. Page 25.

[109] Montessori, Maria. *Creative Development in the Child.* Ed. Rukmini Ramachandran. Vol. 1. Chennai: Kalakshetra, 2007. Print. Pages 180-181.

[110] Montessori, Maria. *The Discovery of the Child.* Trans. Mary A. Johnstone. Chennai: Kalakshetra, 2006. Print. Pages 209-212.

[111] Montessori, Maria. *The Secret of Childhood.* Trans. Barbara B. Carter. Hyderabad: Orient Longman, 2006. Print. Pages 33-41, 124-131.

[112] Montessori, Maria. *The Discovery of the Child.* Trans. Mary A. Johnstone. Chennai: Kalakshetra, 2006. Print. Pages 244-245.

younger peers[113] due to the diminishment or loss of the sensitive periods for order, movement, and sensory perception.[114] Without these three sensitive periods to intrinsically motivate him, the five year old will not likely be as inclined as a three year old to repeat Practical Life and Sensorial activities to the point where concentration and eventually normalization can occur.[115] While this is not to say a five year old cannot be normalized,[116] it is better if a child can begin his Montessori education at two years and ten months of age or just after turning three in order to effortlessly receive all the benefits offered by the prepared environment.[117]

Once a child concentrates upon developmentally appropriate, freely chosen manipulatives that appeal to his sensitive periods in the prepared environment following an initial presentation from the guide, normalization is able to occur. A child's transition from collective stage to normalization is instantaneous, not gradual.[118] As soon as this transformation occurs, all the child's previous deviations, regardless of type, completely disappear and are replaced with behaviors and virtues common to all normalized children:[119] patience, empathy, kindness, compassion, hospitality, pride in one's own accomplishments, happiness for the accomplishments of others, internal discipline, self-regulation, self-confidence, voluntary rejection of external rewards, and the ability to choose and concentrate upon work independently without

---

[113] Montessori, Maria. *The Advanced Montessori Method I*. Vol. 9. Oxford: Clio, 2004. Print. The Clio Montessori Ser. Pages 74-75.

[114] Montessori, Maria. *The Discovery of the Child*. Trans. Mary A. Johnstone. Chennai: Kalakshetra, 2006. Print. Pages 244-245.

[115] Ibid.

[116] Montessori, Maria. *The Advanced Montessori Method I*. Vol. 9. Oxford: Clio, 2004. Print. The Clio Montessori Ser. Pages 74-75.

[117] Montessori, Maria. *Creative Development in the Child*. Ed. Rukmini Ramachandran. Vol. 1. Chennai: Kalakshetra, 2007. Print. Pages 95-101.

[118] Montessori, Maria. *The Absorbent Mind*. Vol. 1. Oxford: Clio, 2004. Print. The Clio Montessori Ser. Page 184.

[119] Ibid. Pages 183-188.

adult interference or guidance. The awakening of normalization also unlocks a child's academic potential as it is only after normalization that a child can apply himself happily and readily to academic work.[120] [121] Normalization therefore provides a necessary stepping stone on the road to a child's independence and readiness for future challenges presented in later years including skills related to positive human relations.[122] Lasting internal and external peace can only occur once normalization is firmly established within every child in the Casa. In short, normalization is an essential prerequisite to fully realized peace.[123]

Disruptions to the Rhythm of the Casa

Despite the provision of a prepared environment, there is no such thing as perfection. While disruptions to the rhythm of the Casa range in magnitude and scope, it is expected that some problems will occur regardless of whether or not normalization in individual students has been achieved. Perhaps one of the largest obstacles to maintaining a peaceful atmosphere is separation anxiety. Every child is unique when it comes to the amount of time it takes to adapt to an unfamiliar environment away from the primary caregiver.[124] Children who are used to attending daycare or who have come from a previous Montessori environment may adapt more readily to life in the Casa than a child who has never been away from home and family. Upon entering a new environment, some children may be uneasy while others may rush

---

[120] Montessori, Maria. *Dr. Montessori's Own Handbook.* Mineola: Dover Publications, 2005. Print. Pages 91-94.

[121] Montessori, Maria. *The Absorbent Mind.* Trans. Claude A. Claremont. Vol. 1. Oxford: Clio, 2004. Print. The Clio Montessori Ser. Page 188.

[122] Ibid. Pages 183-191,202-211.

[123] Ibid. Pages 202, 212-222.

[124] Montessori, Maria. *Creative Development in the Child.* Ed. Rukmini Ramachandran. Vol. 1. Chennai: Kalakshetra, 2007. Print. Pages 179-181.

to embrace the novelty of the Casa and its beautiful manipulatives. Children who are experiencing separation anxiety are likely to cry, so the guide is prepared to reassure him that everything is all right, the parent will return, and they will have a great day together. Depending on the child, the guide may hold his hand and allow the child to follow her or the assistant around the room for a while for security. The guide may then distract him with a fun game or give him some time alone if that suits the child better. Keep in mind that some children want to be hugged while they are crying and some want to be by themselves. Montessori teachers are respectful of individual differences and react accordingly to the needs of each child. Rare cases of severe or ongoing separation anxiety may require making an arrangement with the guide and/or school administrator. In order to avoid traumatizing an extremely anxious child, it may be necessary for one parent to stay in the classroom or school building during the day until the child's confidence and independence blossom.[125] According to Dr. Montessori, the best cure for separation anxiety is patience combined with purposeful work in a loving, supportive, prepared classroom environment. Gradually, even the most timid children focus their attentions upon freely chosen activities and begin their journey toward normalization. When this transformation occurs depends upon the individual child and the guide's expertise.[126] Once a child becomes oriented to his environment and becomes absorbed in freely chosen activities, internal peace begins to develop. Internal peace, the prerequisite to external peace, is only possible once the child feels safe and comfortable in his new environment. Following the acquisition of internal peace, external peace in the form of positive communication skills and overall harmony can occur.[127]

---

[125] Ibid. Page 179.

[126] Ibid. Pages 177-181.

[127] Montessori, Maria. *The Absorbent Mind*. Trans. Claude A. Claremont. Vol. 1. Oxford: Clio, 2004. Print. The Clio Montessori Ser. Pages 183-188, 190, 202-

Besides separation anxiety, far less serious disruptions to the rhythm of the Casa's three hour uninterrupted work period can occur. One such unexpected event can occur in the form of a controversial question initiated by a student. Due to the child-centered nature of the Primary prepared environment, it is not uncommon for a child to spontaneously approach an adult in the room to ask a contentious question such as, "Where do babies come from?" or "Is there really a God?" Rather than pretending the student did not make an inquiry or attempting to silence him, the guide or assistant replies, "That's a good question to ask your parents." This honest, generic response respects the student's family by permitting them to transmit the values they wish to convey to their child. By leaving questions of morality, politics, and religion in the domain of the family rather than the teacher, the adults in the Casa help prevent conflict between parents and teachers that arises from differences in values and opinions.

Although a guide may be required to give a generic reply to a contentious student inquiry, adults in a Montessori environment are careful to never intentionally mislead students or offer fictitious explanations for uncomfortable topics. While presenting fanciful figures such as Santa Claus and the Tooth Fairy as fact may be acceptable in the wider culture, treating fantasy as fact is not in alignment with Montessori's philosophy of preserving a child's inherent dignity by always being honest at an age-appropriate level and respectful. According to Dr. Montessori, it is wrong for adults, including family members, to take advantage of a young child's lack of experience for their own amusement by introducing fanciful figures such as Santa Claus as fact.[128] Beliefs in Santa Claus and other fairy tale characters can also be a source of conflict among students in a classroom. A child who never

---

213.

[128] Montessori, Maria. *The Advanced Montessori Method I*. Vol. 9. Oxford: Clio, 2004. Print. The Clio Montessori Ser. Pages 200, 202-203.

believed in Santa Claus and similar stories may find himself arguing with fellow students who do believe in fairy tales. These types of arguments are difficult to reconcile if the adults in a child's life subscribe to opposite philosophies about the introduction of fantasy as fact. To help provide consistency, and to respect a child's inherent dignity, it is strongly urged that parents of students in a Montessori school resist the temptation to introduce fantasy as fact to their children. While fairy tale figures like Santa Claus may seem like harmless fun, intentionally misleading children erodes the virtues of honesty, trustworthiness, and respect.[129] In addition, presenting fantasy as fact hinders the child's ability to strengthen his intellect to its fullest extent.[130] Keep in mind that Montessori's philosophy of rejecting the introduction of fantasy should not be confused with supporting a child's imagination which is a vital developmental task. The difference between imagination and fantasy is that imagination is created through reality-based experiences in the environment that can be put to practical use[131] whereas fantasy refers to disordered, illusionary thoughts that serve no practical purpose and thereby weaken the child's intellect[132] as well as his ability to effectively act upon his environment.[133] Children depend upon the adults in their lives to lead and guide them toward internal and external peace through the provision of a prepared environment that supports concentration and normalization through freely chosen, developmentally appropriate, hands-on, reality-based work.[134] This acquisition of peace begins with honesty,[135] respect,[136] and

---

[129] Ibid. Page 202.

[130] Ibid. Pages 200, 202-205.

[131] Ibid. Pages 186-197.

[132] Ibid. Pages 186-205.

[133] Montessori, Maria. *Creative Development in the Child.* Ed. Rukmini Ramachandran. Vol. 1. Chennai: Kalakshetra, 2007. Print. Pages 172-177, 180.

[134] Montessori, Maria. *The Absorbent Mind.* Trans. Claude A. Claremont. Vol. 1. Oxford: Clio, 2004. Print. The Clio Montessori Ser. Pages 183-188.

adherence to a philosophy that best supports a young child's holistic development.[137]

Outside of conflicting beliefs, conflicts pertaining to classroom management philosophy between Montessori and traditional classroom settings can become an issue. In the Primary prepared environment, there is no set snack time or bathroom time. Children are free to prepare a snack with ingredients provided in the Casa when hungry, and use the bathroom whenever necessary without seeking permission. An in-class water fountain and restroom are usually provided to facilitate functional independence. Unless mandated by local law, there is no designated nap time as students may rest or sleep on a mat when tired. To protect the dignity of the individual child, permission is never required to perform biological functions. A child who comes from a daycare or school environment where permission is expected prior to performing biological functions may find it difficult to act independently when new to the Casa[138] and ask permission to take a drink of water or use the restroom. The Montessori guide is careful not to encourage permission seeking to perform natural acts within the Casa. If a child who is used to asking permission asks if he may use the bathroom, the guide consistently replies, "You don't need to ask." A child who has been conditioned to seek permission for every action may also ask whether or not he may use a manipulative before taking it from the shelf. If this happens, the guide says something like, "I see that the material you want to use is on the shelf. That means it is

---

[135] Montessori, Maria. *The Advanced Montessori Method I*. Vol. 9. Oxford: Clio, 2004. Print. The Clio Montessori Ser. Pages 202-203.

[136] Montessori, Maria. *The Secret of Childhood*. Trans. Barbara B. Carter. Hyderabad: Orient Longman, 2006. Print. Pages 132-135.

[137] Montessori, Maria. *The Absorbent Mind*. Trans. Claude A. Claremont. Vol. 1. Oxford: Clio, 2004. Print. The Clio Montessori Ser. Pages 183-190, 202-213.

[138] Montessori, Maria. *Creative Development in the Child*. Ed. Rukmini Ramachandran. Vol. 1. Chennai: Kalakshetra, 2007. Print. Pages 170-171.

available for anyone who has had a lesson," or "You don't need to ask to use an available material if you've had a lesson." How the guide responds to the student's question depends upon the circumstance and the individual child. Regardless of how she replies, the guide makes sure that her words effectively convey the fact that the child never needs to ask permission to perform biological functions or carry out certain tasks in the Casa. By protecting the dignity of the child in this manner, the guide promotes functional independence and self-respect, essential qualities for the development of positive human relations for a peaceful environment.

In addition to not encouraging permission seeking, the guide is equally careful not to present herself as the sole source of knowledge in the Casa. If a child has a question about a topic that is appropriate for school, the guide may say, "Let's go look that up together in the encyclopedia." To an older, literate child who is about to transition into elementary school, the guide may encourage the student to do his own research as in, "I think you might find the answer to that question in the encyclopedia." By directing students to outside sources of information, the guide affirms the child's ability to seek answers outside of a single designated source. Knowing how to obtain information outside of the verbal assurances of an authority figure is a vital lifelong skill that lays the foundation for independent thought through self-directed research. When the guide consistently models how to seek information outside of the adult in charge, children learn that their own research is valid. The ability and willingness to seek knowledge independently rather than depending upon a designated person to dictate information broadens a child's intellectual horizon into adulthood, which can ultimately foster understanding between persons and cultures.

Rather than blindly accepting dogma touted by authority figures, a child who knows how to conduct independent research is prepared to question the validity of stated facts in the future by seeking out alternative solutions and sources in order to better understand a situation before making a final decision on how to think or act.[139]

[139] Montessori, Maria. *The Advanced Montessori Method II*. Vol. 13. Oxford: Clio, 2006. Print. The Clio Montessori Ser. Pages 173-180, 195-202.

Part II

Social Relations

Despite occasional disturbances to the flow of the prepared environment, the Casa minimizes such occurrences through its organization. Freedom of movement and work choice within natural limits in the Casa's developmentally appropriate, child-centered environment help prevent conflicts before they occur. When conflicts arise despite preventative measures built into the environment, there are several techniques employed to help restore peace and order to the classroom without resorting to rewards and punishments. These peaceful practices include "Grace and Courtesy" and "The Peace Table."

Grace and Courtesy

Grace and Courtesy, also called "Social Relations," refers to brief skits performed by the guide for small groups of three to seven students to demonstrate manners, classroom procedures, and peaceful conflict resolution. Examples of typical Grace and Courtesy lessons include, "How to Use a Tissue," "What to Say when Someone Is in Your Way," and "How to Carry a Work Rug." Grace and Courtesy presentations are given at the guide's discretion whenever she observes there is a need.

The Origin of Grace and Courtesy

Grace and Courtesy lessons were not created as the result of an educational fad or as an artificially created technique to force children to behave themselves. Rather, the first Grace and

Courtesy lesson was discovered accidentally by Dr. Maria Montessori when entertaining her students with a skit on how to use a handkerchief. At first, Dr. Montessori intended to amuse the children by making sport of her handkerchief, but as the demonstration progressed to the point where she used the handkerchief properly and discreetly, she discovered that her audience expressed great awe and respect in being shown how perform a task correctly. Not only were the children impressed with being shown how to blow their noses properly, they rewarded Dr. Montessori with thunderous applause and effusive thanks for the lesson. In light of her students' reactions, Dr. Montessori realized that children possess an inherent dignity that is often overlooked[140] as well as a strong desire to adopt the manners and practices of the surrounding culture.[141] As a result of these discoveries, Grace and Courtesy lessons have become the primary means of effectively conveying classroom policies in the Casa ever since Dr. Montessori's first handkerchief lesson.

The Meaning of "Grace and Courtesy"

While the term "Grace and Courtesy" may sound archaic, the framework provided by its format is timeless. In order to best understand "Grace and Courtesy," it is necessary to separate the term into its two equally vital components: "grace" and "courtesy." In a Montessori context, "grace" is defined as exercising efficiency and economy of movement. To perform a given task gracefully means to use efficient and relevant movements while avoiding all superfluous actions. In other words, the least amount of movement with the most amount of control is what makes grace possible. A

---

[140] Montessori, Maria. *The Secret of Childhood.* Trans. Barbara B. Carter. Hyderabad: Orient Longman, 2006. Print. Pages 132-133.
[141] Montessori, Maria. *The Absorbent Mind.* Trans. Claude A. Claremont. Vol. 1. Oxford: Clio, 2004. Print. The Clio Montessori Ser. Pages 165-166.

simple example of grace in the Casa and wider culture is the ability to carry a pitcher of water from one location to another. In order to carry a pitcher of water without spilling its contents, a person must enact specific movements and inhibit others which are not relevant to the task of carrying a pitcher. The ability to inhibit superfluous movements requires a great amount of internal control as well as strongly developed gross and fine motor coordination. If the person can exercise enough coordination required to move the pitcher from one point to another without dropping the pitcher or spilling its contents, that person has demonstrated the ability to be graceful in that particular task. While carrying a pitcher of water from one point to another with grace is a simple task for an adult, the level of coordination required to perform this action can be overwhelming to a young, inexperienced child. When a young child has not yet developed the necessary gross and fine motor control to perform a task gracefully, he may appear clumsy to his far more experienced adult counterpart. In the Montessori Casa, the adult's job is not to criticize or otherwise punish poor coordination but to give the child the means to improve his gracefulness through careful modeling and guided practice.

Since "grace" is defined as performing actions efficiently using relevant movements, then "courtesy" is defined as performing actions efficiently using relevant movements toward others. Unlike grace, courtesy extends beyond the ability to perform a task with a high level of coordination while inhibiting superfluous actions. Courtesy is the ability to act positively toward others using the skills acquired by practicing graceful actions. When the words "grace" and "courtesy" are combined, it can be said that courtesy is graceful movement that is directed toward others in a positive way. When the guide helps students direct graceful movement toward others in a positive way through positively phrased reminders and Grace and Courtesy lessons, good manners are naturally reinforced and developed to promote peaceful interactions among everyone in the environment.[142]

Why Grace and Courtesy?

Starting on the first day of school, Grace and Courtesy lessons are all that is needed in the Casa to provide effective classroom management throughout the year. Since children under the age of six or seven have absorbent minds rather than reasoning minds, they absorb the positive and negative influences of the surrounding culture without filters, much like a sponge.[143] Without a reasoning mind, which typically does not exist until a child reaches the Second Plane of Development, lectures, fables, empathy training, and other moralistic methods of inducing desired behavior are completely ineffective.[144] In addition to being incapable of understanding morality before the age of six or seven,[145] young children are also unresponsive to a litany of classroom rules and expectations established during the first day or week of school as they can only internalize proper behaviors and actions by physically practicing them.[146] Since traditional means of establishing classroom rules and expectations are out of the question for an audience consisting entirely of First Plane children, Grace and Courtesy[147] applied within a prepared environment that fosters normalization is the best technique for naturally bringing peace and order to a Montessori Primary Casa.[148]

---

[142] Montessori, Maria. *The Discovery of the Child.* Trans. Mary A. Johnstone. Chennai: Kalakshetra, 2006. Print. Pages 78-81.

[143] Montessori, Maria. *Creative Development in the Child.* Ed. Rukmini Ramachandran. Vol. 1. Chennai: Kalakshetra, 2007. Print. Pages 222-229.

[144] Montessori, Maria. *The Absorbent Mind.* Trans. Claude A. Claremont. Vol. 1. Oxford: Clio, 2004. Print. The Clio Montessori Ser. Pages 175-177, 190.

[145] Ibid. Page 190.

[146] Montessori, Maria. *Creative Development in the Child.* Ed. Rukmini Ramachandran. Vol. 1. Chennai: Kalakshetra, 2007. Print. Pages 64-65.

[147] Montessori, Maria. *The Discovery of the Child.* Trans. Mary A. Johnstone. Chennai: Kalakshetra, 2006. Print. Pages 73-86.

[148] Montessori, Maria. *Education for a New World.* Vol. 5. Oxford: Clio, 2005. Print. The Clio Montessori Ser. Pages 61-69.

Why Grace and Courtesy Works

Grace and Courtesy is effective in the Primary Casa because it appeals to the young child's intrinsic desire to emulate the manners and practices of his surrounding culture[149] in a way that satisfies his inherent dignity,[150] fulfills his need to act upon the environment, and assists him in his continuous quest for knowledge.[151] Young children have an innate and intense desire to adopt the behaviors of the people around them but are often never shown how to perform a given task correctly or how to exhibit a certain cultural courtesy in a way that makes sense to a non-reasoning mind. In order to act appropriately, a child must first be given a simple demonstration in how a given situation should be handled isolated from the incident itself. It is of no help to a child's individual and cultural development if an adult says, "Say, 'thank you!'" or "What do you say!?" in the midst of an incident.[152] Manners are developed not through correction at the moment of the infraction but through careful modeling which removes all obstacles and distractions to best support successful skill acquisition.[153] Unlike punishments and rewards, Grace and Courtesy fosters desired behavior by giving children a safe, comfortable place to practice manners and common procedures isolated from all other tasks. By modeling a single aspect of positive social relations during each Grace and Courtesy lesson to small groups of students and then inviting individual students to

---

[149] Montessori, Maria. *The Absorbent Mind*. Trans. Claude A. Claremont. Vol. 1. Oxford: Clio, 2004. Print. The Clio Montessori Ser. Pages 165-166.

[150] Montessori, Maria. *The Secret of Childhood*. Trans. Barbara B. Carter. Hyderabad: Orient Longman, 2006. Print. Pages 132-135.

[151] Montessori, Maria. *The Absorbent Mind*. Trans. Claude A. Claremont. Vol. 1. Oxford: Clio, 2004. Print. The Clio Montessori Ser. Pages 156-174.

[152] Ibid. Page 190.

[153] Montessori, Maria. *The Secret of Childhood*. Trans. Barbara B. Carter. Hyderabad: Orient Longman, 2006. Print. Page 149.

practice the modeled skill, the guide removes any ambiguity regarding expected proper behavior in a non-threatening, engaging manner that is also entertaining. Once a child masters a skill by practicing it during several repetitions of a given Grace and Courtesy lesson, he can apply what he has learned outside of the context of the lesson in the Casa and wider world[154] to help create a peaceful environment for everyone.[155]

Grace and Courtesy Basics

Grace and Courtesy lessons are based upon need and culture rather than an arbitrarily determined, official list of expectations. Beginning on the first day of school, the guide should keep a written list of anticipated essential Grace and Courtesy lessons to present to students in her class. Common Grace and Courtesy lessons that may be introduced on the first day of school include "How to Use a Tissue for Your Nose," "What to Say When Someone Is in Your Way," "How to Walk around a Work Rug," and "How to Observe a Classmate at Work." In addition to planning lessons for the first days of school, the guide also anticipates lessons that are applicable to particular upcoming circumstances, such as cold and flu season. Before disease begins to spread, the guide gives Grace and Courtesy lessons that include "What to Do if You Have to Sneeze," "What to Do if You Have to Cough," "What to Do after You Blow Your Nose," and "How to Offer Someone a Tissue." These are basic examples of an infinite list of Grace and Courtesy lessons that may arise during the course of a school year. If the guide observes an unexpected negative behavior, she must create a Grace and Courtesy lesson to

---

[154] Montessori, Maria. *Creative Development in the Child.* Ed. Rukmini Ramachandran. Vol. 1. Chennai: Kalakshetra, 2007. Print. Pages 109-112.
[155] Montessori, Maria. *The Absorbent Mind.* Trans. Claude A. Claremont. Vol. 1. Oxford: Clio, 2004. Print. The Clio Montessori Ser. Pages 157, 165-174.

encourage a positive replacement for the observed infraction. For example, if a student develops a sassy attitude toward suggestions given by an adult in the room, the guide needs to think of something positive the child should say when confronted with a constructive correction. In some Casas, a particular lesson about what to say when someone offers a correction may not be necessary. In other Casas, such a lesson may be essential. Beyond universal Grace and Courtesy lessons that help maintain safety, peace, and order in the environment, presentations can vary considerably among classrooms based upon the guide's observations of behaviors in her class. What is important to remember is that any negative behavior observed in a child through six years of age can be addressed through a Grace and Courtesy lesson rather than enacting a system of rewards and punishments due to a young child's innate desire to adopt his surrounding culture and its mores.[156]

Good behavior is a continuous expectation of all children in the Casa. Unlike other behavior programs, Grace and Courtesy lessons are given throughout the year based upon observed need rather than during an adult-imposed schedule. In accordance with the universal expectation of positive, pro-social behavior at all times, the Montessori guide does not create a set schedule to present a "Skill of the Week" or "Skill of the Month" such as respect, kindness, sharing, and so forth. A Grace and Courtesy lesson may be presented at any time during the uninterrupted three hour work period when needed to model proper behavior, classroom expectations, and peaceful conflict resolution skills.

Grace and Courtesy lessons are not designed to teach virtues. Empathy training, *Aesop's Fables*, and other blatant attempts to make children adopt virtues such as patience, kindness, empathy, hospitality, and so on are not part of the Montessori Primary curriculum as morality cannot be successfully taught to First Plane

---

[156] Ibid.

children who have not yet developed reasoning minds.[157] Children under the age of six or seven acquire these internal qualities through normalization, the process in which a child spontaneously abandons all negative behaviors in exchange for positive behaviors.[158] Normalization is not attained through lecturing, storytelling, modeling, or even Grace and Courtesy lessons. Instead, normalization is awakened through concentration upon developmentally appropriate, freely chosen, individual, hands-on work in a prepared environment[159] that provides a minimum three hour uninterrupted work period. While normalization is not an essential prerequisite for a child to adopt the behaviors modeled through Grace and Courtesy lessons,[160] normalization is essential for the virtues of empathy, kindness, hospitality, self-regulation, diligence, and so forth to become fully integrated within the child's burgeoning personality.[161] It is only after normalization has been achieved that a child can internally acquire the virtues that make social life harmonious.[162]

Types of Grace and Courtesy Lessons

While Grace and Courtesy lessons vary from Casa to Casa, all Grace and Courtesy presentations can be organized into three basic categories: good manners, common procedures, and peaceful conflict resolution. Although Grace and Courtesy lessons can be categorized as good manners, common procedures, and peaceful conflict resolution, there is overlap between and among groups. These three classifications, while helpful for the guide's

---

[157] Ibid. Page 190.

[158] Ibid. Pages 182-188.

[159] Ibid.

[160] Ibid. Pages 157, 165-174.

[161] Ibid. Pages 182-188.

[162] Ibid. Page 188.

organizational purposes, are not disclosed to her students. When a guide presents a Grace and Courtesy lesson, she is careful not to provide any superfluous information that would likely confuse the children. As far as the children are concerned, Grace and Courtesy lessons are merely interesting small group presentations. Following are brief explanations and examples of each type of Grace and Courtesy lesson for parent and teacher reference.

Lessons in good manners model respectful communication with others in order to create and maintain a pro-social environment. Examples of manners lessons include "What to Say when Someone Is in Your Way," "What to Say if Someone Offers You Something," and "How to Invite Someone to Have a Conversation." Knowing what to say during common situations helps children behave appropriately without being humiliated by the common, vague adult response, "What do you say?" By learning manners isolated from an incident that requires their use, children have the opportunity to practice specific courteous phrases such as, "Thank you" and "Excuse me" before they need to be used. Once a child internalizes cultural niceties through Grace and Courtesy lessons in good manners, he can apply what he has learned to situations that arise in the Casa and wider world.[163]

Procedural Grace and Courtesy lessons foster functional independence by illustrating how to carry out certain tasks in the Casa and outside world safely, gracefully, and courteously. Examples of procedural lessons include "How to Carry a Chair," "How to Walk around a Work Rug," and "How to Pour a Glass of Water." In addition to using objects correctly, procedural Grace and Courtesy lessons also include practices which help prevent the spread of disease such as "How to Use a Tissue for Your Nose," "What to Do if You Have to Sneeze" and "What to Do if You Have to Cough." These types of procedural lessons also overlap with manners lessons as knowing how to sneeze and cough into a

---

[163] Ibid. Pages 157, 165-174.

sleeve if a tissue is not readily available instead of into the air promotes self-control and shows respect for others. Procedural lessons also demonstrate unobtrusive and helpful behaviors such as "How to Observe Someone's Work" and "How to Ask Someone if He Would Like Some Help to Carry a Table." These types of lessons in common classroom procedures also involve manners as both movement and positive communication skills are necessary to carry out the demonstrated tasks in a safe, unobtrusive, pro-social manner that respects others.

Peaceful conflict resolution, the final category of Grace and Courtesy, gives children the verbal tools they need to defend themselves against disruptive peers and how to engage in diplomacy. Examples of conflict resolution Grace and Courtesy lessons include "What to Say if Someone Is Standing Too Close to Your Work," "What to Say if Someone Hurts Your Feelings," "What to Say if Someone Hurts You," and "What to Say if Someone Calls You a Name You Don't Like." These types of situations are handled through the use of the Three Part Message, a scripted response that allows children to effectively defend themselves with their words. An example of the Three Part Message is described in greater detail later in the chapter under the subheading *"Grace and Courtesy: Conflict Resolution and The Three Part Message."*

Grace and Courtesy Presentations:

General Technique

Like all other presentations in the Casa, Grace and Courtesy lessons are not restricted to an arbitrarily determined time. There is no pre-determined "Grace and Courtesy Time" where students must cease their activities to participate in a group exercise at the teacher's convenience. Instead, when the guide wishes to present a

Grace and Courtesy lesson, she seeks out a small number of available students to join her for her presentation. To gather a group of students, the guide begins by identifying a single available child in the Casa. An "available child" means one who is not currently engaged in a productive task. If a child is wandering around the classroom aimlessly or is being disruptive, the guide may calmly approach him and invite him to sit and wait at the location of the impending presentation while she invites other children. Alternatively, if the guide knows the child is not capable of behaving himself long enough to sit and wait for the presentation to begin, she instead has the child follow her around the room while she invites other students. How exactly the guide proceeds to invite her students depends on her long and short term observations of individual students and the current classroom situation.

Once the group of students has been gathered and is seated on the floor, the guide begins her presentation. To keep her presentation as simple as possible, the guide avoids giving long preambles and instead simply names the lesson she is going to present. If the guide is going to present "What to Do When You Have to Sneeze," she says, "I am going to show you what to do when you have to sneeze." The guide then slowly and deliberately performs the actions required for her Grace and Courtesy lesson without commentary. For this particular presentation, the guide moves her arm across her face so that her nose is buried in the inside of her elbow. Once her arm is in position, she sneezes into her sleeve once or twice. After sneezing, she unfurls her arm to bring it back to its original position. Her demonstration complete, the guide then invites an individual student to practice the skill she just modeled. When choosing a student to practice the skill in front of the group, the guide is careful not to select a child who is shy or one who would perform the task incorrectly on purpose as a joke. She instead chooses an experienced child to take the first turn by saying something like, "Show us what to do when you have to sneeze, (Name)." After the child demonstrates how to sneeze into his sleeve, the guide may invite another child to demonstrate. It is not necessary for the guide to invite every single child to have a turn especially if there are students in the group who are particularly shy or would misbehave if given the opportunity. If a child who was skipped says he did not get a turn, the guide may invite him to practice with her one-on-one after the other children are dismissed. This way, every child who wants a turn has a turn without the danger of embarrassment or causing a disruption.

After the children have finished taking turns demonstrating how to sneeze into their sleeves, the guide concludes her presentation with a brief verbal summary of the completed lesson. The Grace and Courtesy lesson summary for sneezing into a sleeve may sound like this: "Now you know what to do when you have to sneeze." When the presentation is complete, the guide dismisses the students in her group one at a time to maintain an orderly, peaceful atmosphere. To dismiss an individual student, the guide says, "What would you like to do next, (Name)?" If the child knows what he would like to do, he is free to leave the group to move on to his chosen task. While the child is walking toward his next work, it may be beneficial for the guide to casually chat with the other children about his work choice as in, "Oh, I see that (Name) is going over to the shelf. What did he say he was going to do again? ... That's right! He's going to work with the Pink Tower!" Although it is not required that the guide wait until the dismissed child is working before dismissing the next student, it can help prevent disputes over materials. If the guide were to dismiss a student who said he wanted to work with the Pink Tower, and then asked the next student what he wants to do before the first student actually made it to the Pink Tower, the second child may say, "I want to work with the Pink Tower!" This could then cause a conflict between the two students in a race for the Pink Tower, a conflict that could have been easily avoided by not dismissing the second student until the first student has chosen his work. Waiting to dismiss the second child until the first child has chosen his work also establishes some accountability within the first child as the other children are waiting for him to carry out the work he said he was going to do. Naturally, there is no obligation for the first child to actually choose the work he originally decided upon as freedom of work choice still applies in this situation. Regardless of whether or not the first student actually uses the Pink Tower as planned, the delay between dismissing each student from the group helps reduce the likelihood of conflicts over a particular material's use.

When a guide is dismissing individual students from her group, it is common for a number of children to not know what they want to do next. In this case, the guide tells the child to take some time to think about it, and then asks the next child in the group what he would like to do next. Once all the children who know what they want to do have been dismissed, the guide has the undecided students stand up and follow her as she gives a tour of the classroom's available materials. To help motivate her students, the guide slowly and systematically walks from shelf to shelf with the children in tow as she names the materials she sees. The guide's tour may sound something like this: "Let's see. I see some Dressing Frames that are available. And over here we have Hand Washing. And what's this down here? Oh, I see that Washing a Chalkboard is also available..." As the guide gives her tour of the materials, a child will often see a manipulative of interest in which he has had a lesson. When this happens, he is free to select the material and take it to a table or work rug. The guide then continues to suggest materials to her remaining group of students until they each find individual work. If a student still cannot think of something to do after the guide makes suggestions, the guide may invite him to another group activity, lead him in a Facilitated Conversation, or just give the child some time alone to think about what he would like to do next. How the guide handles the situation depends upon the individual child and the circumstances. If the child still cannot figure out what to do after receiving multiple suggestions for individual activities, the guide may tell the child to "take some time to think about it," and then excuse herself to do other work. It is important to remember that a child does not need to do individual work in the Casa every minute. Instead, he may be inclined to observe fellow classmates at work following the guide's Grace and Courtesy lesson. Sometimes, a child may just be seeking the emotional security of being near the guide for a while. If the child is seeking emotional security, he is free to follow the guide as she goes about her work but may not interrupt her while she is giving presentations or making observations for her records. After a while, the child may find it boring to hang around the busy guide and find individual work. Every child is different. What is important is that the guide remains present for the emotional security of her students[164] but not so available that the children become too dependent upon her for their learning and entertainment.[165] [166] Eventually, when a student is normalized, he will naturally attach himself to individual work rather than the guide or her assistant.[167] It is only after a student is normalized through concentration upon developmentally appropriate, freely chosen, hands-on, individual work that inner peace can develop as a prerequisite to external peace for the betterment of all.[168]

Following each Grace and Courtesy lesson, the guide makes a note in her records that includes the date and time of the

---

[164] Ibid. Pages 247, 255-257.

[165] Montessori, Maria. *Creative Development in the Child*. Ed. Rukmini Ramachandran. Vol. 1. Chennai: Kalakshetra, 2007. Print. Pages 180-183.

[166] Montessori, Maria. *The Secret of Childhood*. Trans. Barbara B. Carter. Hyderabad: Orient Longman, 2006. Print. Pages 167-168.

[167] Montessori, Maria. *The Child, Society, and the World: Unpublished Speeches and Writings*. Vol. 7. Oxford: Clio, 2006. Print. The Clio Montessori Ser. Pages 17-18.

[168] Montessori, Maria. *The Absorbent Mind*. Trans. Claude A. Claremont. Vol. 1. Oxford: Clio, 2004. Print. The Clio Montessori Ser. Pages 183-191, 202-214.

presentation. She also notes the number of times the lesson has been presented. It is not necessary for her to note individual student participants in her records unless a child is in particular need of a specific Grace and Courtesy lesson because repetition of the lesson increases exposure to the entire class over a period of time. Since young children effortlessly absorb the entire atmosphere of the Casa via osmosis due to the power of the absorbent mind, students who did not attend a particular lesson will still be exposed to it simply due to their presence in the classroom.[169]

Important Grace and Courtesy Considerations

It is essential to remember that Grace and Courtesy is an age-appropriate means of modeling manners, procedures, and peaceful conflict resolution skills to young children, not a punishment. If a child in the Casa misbehaves or otherwise fails to follow a procedure correctly, the guide is careful to never single him out for a Grace and Courtesy lesson, nor will she draw attention to him at the moment of the infraction. Instead, the guide may distract the disruptive student with an individual or small group activity. This gives the guide time to take note of the infraction so that she may plan to give an appropriate Grace and Courtesy lesson later in the day isolated from the actual incident. Exactly how the guide responds to the incident depends upon the individual child, the nature of the infraction, and the current circumstances. If a child carelessly steps on another child's work rug while walking, the guide may not have to intervene immediately, especially if the working child did not notice or complain. In this case, the guide notes the incident and gives a Grace and Courtesy lesson for "How to Walk around a Work Rug" as soon as the opportunity arises. If

---

[169] Montessori, Maria. *The Formation of Man*. Trans. A. M. Joosten. Vol. 3. Amsterdam: Montessori-Pierson, 2007. Print. The Montessori Ser. Pages 61-64.

the child is actively disrupting another student's work, distracting the disruptive child may be the best option. Once again, the guide will know how best to proceed based upon her observations and assessment of each situation. Even if the situation warrants her immediate intervention, a formal Grace and Courtesy lesson will be presented at a time isolated from the actual incident rather than immediately following the infraction. By waiting for an opportune moment to present a Grace and Courtesy lesson rather than enforcing an immediate presentation, the guide maintains the Grace and Courtesy lesson's status as a tool for modeling correct behavior rather than a means of punishment.

When the guide has the opportunity to present the applicable lesson, she invites several children to her presentation including the student who committed the infraction. Once her group is gathered, she presents the Grace and Courtesy lesson using the standard aforementioned technique: 1) verbally introducing the lesson, 2) presenting the lesson, 3) allowing time for individual practice, 4) summarizing the lesson, and 5) dismissing students individually. By adhering to the standard Grace and Courtesy technique in light of a prior incident, the guide models proper behavior without resorting to individual or group punishment. Even though students in addition to the one who committed the infraction are invited to the same Grace and Courtesy lesson, the presentation is treated like any other small group activity. This consistent format prevents the child who was the motivation for the lesson from being singled out. All students attending the presentation, regardless of experience level, benefit from the review of previously mastered Grace and Courtesy lessons. Attending a familiar Grace and Courtesy lesson can actually help a student become more aware of his actions, which may help him become a better role model for his younger peers.[170]

---

[170] Montessori, Maria. *The Absorbent Mind.* Trans. Claude A. Claremont. Vol. 1. Oxford: Clio, 2004. Print. The Clio Montessori Ser. Page 207.

While Grace and Courtesy lessons are used to model polite behavior and actions, it is important to note that such presentations purposely refrain from making students apologize immediately after committing an offense. Forcing a student to say he is "sorry" as an automatic response to an infraction promotes dishonesty and can weaken diplomacy skills.[171] A child who says "sorry" to an infraction as a reflexive response whether he is contrite or not does nothing to resolve the act he has committed. Instead, conflict resolution in Montessori focuses upon how to discuss problems and make amends rather than forcing someone to say he is sorry when he is clearly not. If a child truly regrets his actions, it is only then that he may rightfully offer verbal contrition. True contrition, however, is expressed by making amends and/or coming to a mutually beneficial, pro-social agreement, not meaningless rehearsed phrases. It is only though diplomacy, a skill that develops with time and guided practice, that conflicts between students can be resolved amicably to both parties' mutual satisfaction. The ability to engage in diplomacy begins with students learning how to take turns verbally articulating needs, wants, and limits to their peers in a peaceful, meaningful, and thoughtful manner. Through Grace and Courtesy lessons in manners and conflict resolution, conflicts are resolved rather than shoved aside with an automatic, insincere reply of, "I'm sorry."

Just as Grace and Courtesy lessons are not used to enforce the artificial use of the phrase, "I'm sorry," manners presentations are also not designed to make children say "please" when setting clear limits with others. Although "please" is perfectly appropriate to say when making a request, it is never appropriate when making a demand. For example, if a student disrupts another student's work,

---

[171] Goertz, Donna B. "Did You Say "Sorry?": Seeing Through Montessori Eyes." *Parenting for a New World* XVI.2 (2008). *AMI/USA News*. Association Montessori Internationale, Apr. 2008. Web. 6 Dec. 2014. <http://donnabryantgoertz.com/2013/wp-content/uploads/2014/12/AMI-Did-You-Say-Sorry.pdf>.

the child who is being bothered should say, "You can step away from my work," not, "Please step away from my work." By saying, "You can step away from my work" to a disruptive child, the student who is being bothered is setting a clear, precise limit that the other student must respect. "Please step away from my work," sounds like an open-ended request that does not carry the necessary weight for the student to verbally defend himself against an unwanted intrusion. This is not to say that "please" is not used in the Casa. Any situation which involves a request would warrant the use of "please" as in, "Will you please help me move this table?" For the sake of personal safety, personal space, good manners, diplomacy, and external peace, it is essential that children learn at a young age the appropriate times to use "please" as opposed to emphatically stating a clear, concise, non-negotiable limit. Grace and Courtesy lessons aid students in understanding and applying this vital distinction to help create and support a peaceful environment optimal for individual and social life.

Just as important as using the proper Grace and Courtesy technique are patience and repetition. Every Grace and Courtesy lesson, no matter how basic, must be repeated multiple times throughout the school year for maximum effectiveness. One Grace and Courtesy lesson is never enough to encourage proper, pro-social, peaceful behavior. During the beginning of the school year, it is not uncommon for a particular Grace and Courtesy lesson to be repeated several times within the same three hour uninterrupted work period for several days in succession. The guide must be patient and constantly model the demonstrated behaviors in order for her students to internalize the positive culture of the Casa. In Montessori, there are no double standards for teacher and student behavior. Only if the adults in the Montessori environment consistently and tirelessly model expected behaviors both inside and outside of formal Grace and Courtesy lessons in addition to offering manipulatives to foster concentration and eventually normalization can children fully integrate positive communication and actions into their daily lives to help create a peaceful atmosphere for themselves and others.[172]

Grace and Courtesy: Manners

Good manners help create a peaceful, pleasant environment for everyone. To present a Grace and Courtesy lesson pertaining to good manners, the guide begins by employing the general Grace and Courtesy technique. In the case of a manners presentation, it is sometimes necessary for the guide to set up props or ask the aide or an older student for assistance before inviting children to attend the lesson. For the lesson "What to Say When Someone Is in Your Way," the guide requires the help of one adult or child who will act as the person who is in the guide's way. It is often better if the guide can employ the help of an older, experienced student rather than her adult assistant for her presentation as the children in attendance may be more likely to follow the example of a slightly older peer rather than an adult due to the proximity of ages between the children in the group and their assisting older classmate. In addition, the child assistant also gains the experience of acting as a positive role model for his younger peers.[173]

After selecting a willing and able assistant for the impending Grace and Courtesy lesson, the guide enacts a brief rehearsal period to establish the appropriate context for the presentation. To make the skit as clear and convincing as possible, the guide has the assistant stand in a manner that creates an obstruction which makes it impossible for the guide to pass through without saying, "Excuse me." She then tells the assistant what to say and do when she says,

---

[172] Montessori, Maria. *The Child, Society, and the World: Unpublished Speeches and Writings*. Vol. 7. Oxford: Clio, 2006. Print. The Clio Montessori Ser. Pages 12-19.

[173] Montessori, Maria. *The Absorbent Mind*. Trans. Claude A. Claremont. Vol. 1. Oxford: Clio, 2004. Print. The Clio Montessori Ser. Pages 206-207.

"Excuse me." The guide and assistant practice the scene a few times until achieving the desired effect. Once the scene is ready, the guide invites her group of students individually as with any other Grace and Courtesy presentation.

After the children are seated, the guide gives her brief verbal introduction as in, "I am going to show you what to do when someone is in your way." She then approaches the child or adult aide who is in her way and says, "Excuse me." The assistant says, "Certainly," and then steps aside so the guide can pass. Following this brief demonstration, the guide has the assistant return to his original position. Once the scene is reset, the guide invites individual students to practice walking up to the assistant and saying, "Excuse me," so the student may pass. When the first student has finished taking a turn, the assistant once again returns to his original position so the next child can practice saying, "Excuse me" before passing through.

Following individual practice, the guide summarizes her lesson by saying, "Now you know what to do when someone is in your way." The guide then dismisses students one at a time in the usual fashion. She also thanks and dismisses her assistant. Once everyone is dismissed, the guide notes the lesson in her records and moves on to her next task.

Grace and Courtesy: Common Procedures

The ability to safely and effectively enact common procedures in the Casa promotes gross and fine motor control as well as functional independence. To present a Grace and Courtesy lesson for a common procedure, the guide gathers any necessary props and/or assistants before gathering a small group of students. Not every procedural Grace and Courtesy lesson requires props or assistants. Lessons such as "What to Do When You Have to Sneeze" and "What to Do When You Have to Cough" do not require props or assistants whereas lessons such as "How to Move a Table" require an actual table and one assistant to help move it. Other presentations, such as "How to Carry a Work Rug," require a prop but no assistants.

To present the lesson "How to Carry a Work Rug," the guide gathers her group of students one at a time near a rolled work rug. The guide says, "I am going to show you how to carry a work rug." After giving her introduction, the guide carefully picks up the rolled rug by wrapping her hands around its middle making sure one hand is placed above the other. Holding the rug close to her body, she takes a few slow steps, looks both ways before changing directions, carefully walks a few more steps, looks both ways again, returns to her original location, and then gently puts the rug back where it belongs. Following her demonstration, she invites individual students to carry the work rug as demonstrated. Once the selected children have taken their turns, the guide verbally summarizes the lesson by saying, "Now you know how to carry a work rug." She then dismisses the students individually. Following dismissal, the guide notes the presentation in her records before resuming her other work.

Grace and Courtesy:

Conflict Resolution and the Three Part Message

When a minor behavioral incident occurs, such as a child disturbing a classmate's work, the guide distracts the disruptive child by showing him something interesting. The guide notes the behavior in her records and gives an appropriate Grace and Courtesy lesson as soon as the opportunity arises. In most cases, this is sufficient to bring peace and order to the Casa. When more serious offenses such as hitting or biting occur, the "Three Part Message" is used to stop the behavior. The Three Part Message is a clear, direct, immediate verbal response to an infraction that names the problem, says what you want the instigator to do, and makes it clear you do not want the behavior to be repeated. This message can be delivered by the guide or another student depending on the situation. Early in the year, the guide gives a Grace and Courtesy lesson on how to use the Three Part Message to give students the verbal tools they need to defend themselves should a serious incident arise. There are several examples of the Three Part Message that may be demonstrated during a Grace and Courtesy lesson including "What to Say When Someone Hurts You," "What to Say When Someone Calls You a Name You Don't Like," and "What to Say When Someone Hurts Your Feelings."

To present the Grace and Courtesy lesson "What to Say When Someone Hurts You," the guide gathers her group of students individually in the usual manner. An assistant is optional during this presentation as the guide models only how to respond to a negative situation rather than present the situation itself. Once the students are gathered, the guide gives a verbal introduction as in, "I'm going to show you what to do if someone hurts you." The guide then verbally demonstrates the Three Part Message by naming the undesired behavior, concisely saying what she thinks about it, and what she wants the instigator to do. If the guide is using an assistant to demonstrate, she delivers the Three Part Message to her assistant, who remains silent throughout the presentation. If an assistant is not present, the guide delivers the Three Part Message aloud in a way that implies she is speaking to someone. During the Grace and Courtesy lesson, her deliverance of the Three Part Message may be general as in, "You hurt me! I don't like that! Don't hurt me again!" or as specific as, "You hit me! That hurt! Don't hit me again!" Whether the Three Part Message is general or specific, the guide walks away to model that the child should walk away from the instigator after delivering the message. If necessary, the guide may give a verbal point of interest that after walking away, the child should tell the teacher what happened.

After demonstrating walking away following verbal delivery of the Three Part Message, the guide returns to the group and invites individual students to stand up and practice delivering the Three Part Message complete with the conclusion where they walk away from the perpetrator. Following individual practice, the guide summarizes her lesson by saying, "Now you know what to do when someone hurts you." She then dismisses students individually in the usual manner. Once all students have been dismissed, the guide notes the lesson in her records and moves on to other work.

Why the Three Part Message Works

Usually the Three Part Message is enough to stop behavior problems in the Casa because children under the age of six generally strive to be like the people around them. If a child behaves badly and people walk away from him because of it, his behavior will change quickly.[174] [175] Knowing how to use the Three Part Message enables a student to defend himself with his words and set clear limits, important prerequisites to more advanced peaceful conflict resolution skills. As the year progresses, children rely less on teachers and other adults to settle their conflicts. Instead, they learn how to settle disputes through positive phrasing and diplomacy. This is usually seen in the form of a "Peace Table." The Peace Table is a place in the Casa where children who are having a disagreement can meet and take turns explaining their sides of the story. Early experiences at the Peace Table may require assistance from the teacher as a mediator, but children

---

[174] Montessori, Maria. *The Discovery of the Child.* Trans. Mary A. Johnstone. Chennai: Kalakshetra, 2006. Print. Page 85.

[175] Montessori, Maria. *The Absorbent Mind.* Vol. 1. Oxford: Clio, 2004. Print. The Clio Montessori Ser. Pages 208-211.

should eventually be able to solve their own problems with little or no adult help.

Conflict Resolution and The Peace Table

When conflicts between students arise in the Montessori Casa, the guide does not become an autocratic rule enforcer who settles disputes by issuing punishments from on high as though she were the judge and jury of the classroom. Instead, when inexperienced students get into an argument, the guide intervenes as a mediator who listens to both sides of the story even if she saw precisely what happened. To mediate effectively, the guide makes sure the children who are having a conflict do not speak over one another. The guide also listens to both students' perspectives without interrupting. When there is a lull in the conversation, the guide does her best to help the students reach a joint amicable solution through dialogue. The nature of the solution depends entirely upon the individual circumstance. If the children were arguing because they disagreed about a contentious topic such as the existence of Santa Claus, the guide may say, "It sounds like you disagree, and that's okay. This is one of those times when you can agree to disagree. And after you agree to disagree, you can walk away and do something else." In many cases, dropping the issue by agreeing to disagree may be the best solution. Following an incident of this nature, the guide may prepare a Grace and Courtesy lesson about how to agree to disagree.

During a more intense encounter, such as a student calling another student a name he disliked, the guide may coach the offended child to use the Three Part Message as in, "You called me a name I didn't like. My name is (Name). That's what you can call me." Usually this is enough for the offending child to change his behavior. The issue is then dropped and life in the Casa moves on. Following the incident, the guide may introduce or review a

Grace and Courtesy lesson on how to use the Three Part Message if someone calls you a name you dislike.

With young, inexperienced students, a high level of adult mediation during a conflict is often necessary to reach a peaceful resolve. As the year progresses, however, students learn how to peaceably resolve their own conflicts with increasingly limited adult mediation by using The Peace Table, an area in the Casa where students can civilly discuss their disputes and negotiate a mutually beneficial solution. Like all other materials and activities in the Casa, The Peace Table requires a presentation from the guide followed by practice. How The Peace Table is introduced may vary slightly by Casa and by individual circumstances. While The Peace Table may be presented during a Grace and Courtesy lesson, it may also be introduced casually as a point of interest during the heat of a conflict depending upon the situation. It is also important to keep in mind that different Montessori lineages, or styles of Montessori training, enact slightly different practices when it comes to implementing The Peace Table. Some Montessori Casas have an official Peace Table in the classroom at all times whereas other Casas use any available table as The Peace Table only when the need arises. Some Casas may use a Peace Rug instead of a Peace Table. Other Casas do not use a physical table or rug at all and treat The Peace Table as a more symbolic concept. In a Casa where a physical Peace Table is absent, an object symbolic of peace such as a small world globe or dove figurine may be used anywhere in the classroom as an inanimate mediator to help resolve student conflicts. In some Casas, the use of The Peace Table is highly ritualized whereas other Casas treat this aspect of conflict resolution more casually. Keep these differences in mind when reading about how The Peace Table is set up and introduced as practices may vary.

The Peace Table Basics

The Peace Table usually consists of a child-sized work table, two chairs seated across from each other, and an object symbolic of peace such as a figurine of a dove placed at the center of the table. The symbolic object acts as an inanimate mediator during the course of a conflict. Whoever is holding the object speaks and whoever is not holding the object must listen silently without interrupting. After the first child speaks, he hands the object to the second child. Once the second child is holding the object, it is his turn to speak without interruption. The object is then passed back and forth in this manner until the children reach an amicable solution. At first, this simple turn taking exercise may require help from an adult mediator. Eventually, the goal is for children to be able to solve their own conflicts at The Peace Table with minimal or no adult assistance.

Presenting The Peace Table

How the guide introduces The Peace Table depends upon her training, experience, observations of the individual situation, and the setup of The Peace Table itself. In a Casa where The Peace Table is present at all times, the guide may introduce its use during a Grace and Courtesy lesson or at the moment of need. If the Casa uses a symbolic object that may be taken to any table to create The Peace Table when necessary, the guide must adjust her lesson accordingly. Following is an example of a Grace and Courtesy lesson that may be presented in a Casa where there is an official Peace Table.

To give a Grace and Courtesy lesson about peaceful conflict resolution in a Casa with a designated Peace Table, the guide may invite an older, experienced student in the classroom to help her give a demonstration on how to use The Peace Table. After the student agrees to help, the guide and child assistant decide upon a scene that would require the use of The Peace Table. An example of a scene could be a conflict about two students wanting to use the same Puzzle Map at the same time. After deciding upon the nature of the conflict, the guide and student rehearse the upcoming presentation. During rehearsal, the guide and child take turns passing the object back and forth while giving their sides of the story. Neither person interrupts the other. When someone is speaking, he uses a calm voice and restricts his comments to facts and feelings rather than resorting to name calling or accusations.

Following the brief rehearsal period, the guide invites individual students to her Grace and Courtesy lesson in the usual manner. Once the students have gathered near The Peace Table, the guide introduces the scene by saying something like, "(Name) and I are going to show you what to do if you have a disagreement with someone." The guide and her student assistant then sit at The Peace Table. The guide holds the object and says something like, "I didn't like it when you took the Puzzle Map of South America because I was going to use it." She hands the object to the student assistant who then replies with his version of the story as in, "The rule is that anyone can take an available material off the shelf if he's had a lesson, and I took it off the shelf first." The child then hands the object back to the guide who continues to give her side of the story. They continue to pass the object back and forth until a solution is reached. The guide's concession may sound like, "Well, I guess I could work with the Brown Stair until you're done with the Puzzle Map of South America. Then I'll take a turn when you're finished." Now that the conflict is resolved, the guide puts the object back in the center of the table. Once the symbolic object is returned to its proper place at the center of the table, the guide and student calmly stand up and walk away. When the guide returns to her student audience, she says, "Now you know what to do when you have a disagreement with someone." Due to the open-ended nature of The Peace Table presentation, the guide may dispense with the student practice period and begin to dismiss students individually. Once the students are dismissed, she thanks the child assistant for helping her, notes the presentation in her records, and then returns to her other work. Additional Peace Table lessons can be given at a later time to reinforce the peaceful conflict resolution skills demonstrated.

In addition to the example just given where the guide models diplomacy during a Grace and Courtesy lesson with the help of a student, the guide can also arrange a Grace and Courtesy lesson where two older students demonstrate how to use The Peace Table. To do this, the guide invites two older, experienced students to help her create a Grace and Courtesy skit on how to use The Peace Table. After a guided rehearsal period, the guide invites a small group of students one at a time to the Grace and Courtesy lesson. This time, the guide introduces the lesson by saying something like, "(Name) and (Name) are going to show you what to do when you have a disagreement with someone." The two children then begin their previously rehearsed demonstration on how to use The Peace Table including how to use the inanimate object as a mediator. When they are finished, the guide concludes the lesson by saying, "Now you know what to do when you have a disagreement with someone." Students are then dismissed individually in the usual manner.

Presenting a Grace and Courtesy lesson is not the only way to introduce The Peace Table. If students are in the middle of an argument, the guide can gently intervene by encouraging the arguing children to come with her to The Peace Table. The guide then helps the students use the object as a concrete reminder to take turns speaking about what happened and how they felt about it. When the conflict is resolved, the children are free to choose work and the guide resumes her business. Usually no further action needs to be taken by the guide once the children reach an amicable solution to their problem.

In a Casa that does not have an official Peace Table, the guide modifies her lessons on peaceful conflict resolution accordingly. Instead of demonstrating how to use The Peace Table, the guide may give a presentation on how to use a peace object as an inanimate mediator at any table. To give a Grace and Courtesy lesson without an official Peace Table, the guide may invite an older student to help her demonstrate how to use the object symbolic of peace. After a student accepts the guide's invitation, the guide and student create a scenario that would require the use of the object. Following the guided rehearsal period, the guide invites students to attend the Grace and Courtesy lesson. Once the students are gathered near the peace object, the guide introduces the presentation by saying something like, "(Name) and I are going to show you what to do when you have a disagreement with someone." The guide then picks up the object from its designated place on the shelf and takes it to a nearby table. She and her child assistant then sit at the table across from each other and use the object as an inanimate mediator in the same manner as it would be used if the Casa had an official Peace Table. As always, whoever is holding the object speaks and whoever is not holding the object listens silently and respectfully until it is his turn to hold the object and speak. The object acting as the inanimate mediator is passed back and forth until a solution is reached. Once the conflict is resolved, the guide takes the object from the table and returns it to its original position on the shelf, ready for the next person to use. To summarize the presentation, the guide says something like, "Now you know what to do when you have a disagreement with someone." She then dismisses each student individually in the typical fashion before noting the presentation in her records and resuming other work.

Regardless of whether or not an individual Casa uses a designated Peace Table, the principles of peaceful conflict resolution remain a constant throughout the Montessori Primary Method. Grace and Courtesy, diplomacy, negotiation, making amends, and resolving differences of opinion by agreeing to disagree rather than issuing rewards and punishments are the tools used to help create and maintain the Casa's peaceful, pro-social environment that supports optimal individual and social development for the betterment of humanity.

Positive Phrasing

Outside of formal Grace and Courtesy lessons and The Peace Table, the Montessori guide seeks to maintain the emotionally healthy atmosphere of the Casa by using positive phrasing. "Positive phrasing" refers to the honest, clear, concise, and respectful manner in which Montessori guides interact with students, parents, and colleagues. In the Casa, positive phrasing is used to foster pro-social student behavior without resorting to negative comments. If a child is standing on a chair, for instance, the guide says something like, "We stand on the floor," instead of, "Don't stand on the chair." By telling a student what to do rather than what not to do, the guide establishes clear limits and expectations that are not open to debate. If the guide used the negative command, "Don't stand on the chair," the child would likely seek other pieces of furniture to stand on such as tables. The guide would then have to make an entire list of rules describing what the child was not allowed to do such as, "Don't stand on the chair. Don't stand on the table. Don't climb on the windowsill," and so forth. The positively phrased, "We stand on the floor" eliminates the need to create extra rules that tell a child what he may not do. Limiting the use of the words "don't" and "no" in the Casa also helps create a safe environment by reserving such powerful, negative words exclusively for emergencies. In the Casa, a sharp, "No!" is only used when a child is about to be in danger. The use of "no" is otherwise strictly limited so that it will retain its power during a true emergency.

In addition to establishing clear rules and expectations,

positive phrasing demonstrates respect for the child and promotes overall harmony in the classroom. Since First Plane children instinctively absorb the surrounding culture,[176] proper behavior established through the combination of positive phrasing, Grace and Courtesy, and concentration upon hands-on, freely chosen work within the prepared environment creates an atmosphere where neither external rewards nor punishments are necessary to ensure peaceful social relations.[177]

Self-Discipline and Natural Consequences

Rewards and punishments are unnecessary in the Montessori Primary Casa as positive phrasing, Grace and Courtesy, and normalization naturally lead to self-discipline.[178] When a child becomes normalized, all his previous negative behaviors disappear instantly[179] and are replaced with positive behaviors and virtues including kindness, empathy, hospitality, and the ability to work joyfully upon freely chosen, independent work without adult interference or guidance. This instant, spontaneous transformation of a young child's personality makes external discipline completely unnecessary.[180] Once the spontaneous inner discipline resulting from normalization is firmly established, a strong foundation has been laid for lasting peace within the classroom which can then be extended to the outside world.[181]

When infractions occur, regardless of whether or not a child is

---

[176] Montessori, Maria. *The Absorbent Mind*. Trans. Claude A. Claremont. Vol. 1. Oxford: Clio, 2004. Print. The Clio Montessori Ser. Pages 157, 165-174.

[177] Montessori, Maria. *The Discovery of the Child*. Trans. Mary A. Johnstone. Chennai: Kalakshetra, 2006. Print. Pages 334-350.

[178] Montessori, Maria. *The Absorbent Mind*. Trans. Claude A. Claremont. Vol. 1. Oxford: Clio, 2004. Print. The Clio Montessori Ser. Pages 182-188.

[179] Ibid. Page 184.

[180] Ibid. Pages 182-188.

[181] Ibid. Pages 182-222.

normalized, natural consequences are used to make amends rather than the issuance of unnatural punishments such as "time-outs." In Montessori, there are no "time-outs" for negative behavior for two basic reasons. First, a time-out is not a natural follow-up to an infraction. If a child breaks a dish, for example, in what way is a time-out an appropriate reaction to the situation? Not only is such a punishment irrational for the incident, it wounds the child's dignity and does nothing to repair the broken dish. Second, time-outs make no sense to a young child as children under the age of six or seven are incapable of being taught morality.[182] To issue a time-out therefore does nothing to improve the child's character or behavior as he is incapable of understanding its alleged purpose to somehow cure him of the infraction he committed.[183] Furthermore, a time-out provides no opportunity for the child to develop self-discipline.[184] In the case of the broken dish, the most logical natural consequence is for the child to help clean up the pieces under careful adult supervision. At a later time, the guide may present a Grace and Courtesy lesson to demonstrate how to carry a dish in a way that it is less likely to fall and break. By using a natural consequence rather than a punishment, no one is humiliated, the child's inherent dignity is protected, and the problem is resolved.

In the case of intentional infractions, such as a child pushing another child, natural consequences are also applied instead of punishments. A natural consequence in this case may be that the child who was pushed delivers the Three Part Message to the first child before walking away to tell the teacher what happened. For a First Plane child, this is usually enough to stop the behavior in the future as the offending student receives the message that no one wants to play with him or talk to him if he is too rough or

---

[182] Ibid. Pages 190-191.
[183] Ibid. Pages 180-191.
[184] Montessori, Maria. *Education for a New World*. Vol. 5. Oxford: Clio, 2005. Print. The Clio Montessori Ser. Pages 61-66.

otherwise unpleasant. As a follow-up to the incident, the guide may introduce applicable Grace and Courtesy lessons such as "What to Do When Someone Is in Your Way." If necessary, the guide may also encourage the quarreling students to resolve their dispute peacefully at The Peace Table. These natural consequences help the child acquire and exercise self-discipline unlike a time-out which does nothing to help the child improve his character.[185] As the child develops self-discipline through natural consequences and normalization, internal peace is able to emerge as a precursor to external peace and eventually social cohesion.[186]

Social Cohesion

Social cohesion, originally called "cohesion in the social unit,"[187] refers to the process in which normalized children in the Montessori prepared environment spontaneously form a community where each student wants not only to do well for himself but is proud of the accomplishments of his fellow classmates.[188] In a Casa where social cohesion has successfully developed, cooperation with others for the benefit of all, not competition, becomes the instinct of every student in the classroom.[189] [190] It is important to note that social cohesion is not developed as the result of an external force such as the teacher enforcing positive behaviors. Rather, social cohesion is the direct result of normalization,[191] the process in which a child abandons

---

[185] Montessori, Maria. *The Absorbent Mind*. Trans. Claude A. Claremont. Vol. 1. Oxford: Clio, 2004. Print. The Clio Montessori Ser. Page 182.

[186] Ibid. Pages 182-222.

[187] Ibid. Page 212.

[188] Ibid. Page 213.

[189] Ibid. Pages 206-207, 213.

[190] Montessori, Maria. *The Child, Society, and the World: Unpublished Speeches and Writings*. Vol. 7. Oxford: Clio, 2006. Print. The Clio Montessori Ser. Pages 21-28.

all negative behaviors in exchange for positive behaviors including kindness, patience, and empathy.[192] Since normalization directly causes the acquisition of virtues that make harmonious social life among young children possible,[193] it is appropriate to say that social cohesion is established first and foremost through the conditions of the Primary prepared environment that permit normalization to occur.[194] The combination of the developmentally appropriate mixed-age groups of children, the full set of Primary manipulatives, and the trained Montessori guide within the Casa's three hour uninterrupted work period foster concentration upon freely chosen, hands-on, cognitively appropriate, individual activities. Concentration upon purposeful work in the prepared environment leads to normalization, an essential foundation for internal and external peace.[195] Fully realized peace in the Casa ultimately manifests itself through social cohesion wherein every student genuinely cares about his community of peers and seeks to act in a manner that best supports positive social relations for lasting peace.[196]

Fostering Social Cohesion

When considering social cohesion as a natural development in normalized children, it helps to think of the Casa as its own pro-social culture that seeks to prevent conflicts through its policy of

---

[191] Montessori, Maria. *The Absorbent Mind.* Trans. Claude A. Claremont. Vol. 1. Oxford: Clio, 2004. Print. The Clio Montessori Ser. Pages 212-222.
[192] Ibid. Pages 182-188.
[193] Ibid. Pages 182-188, 190, 202-222.
[194] Montessori, Maria. *The Child, Society, and the World: Unpublished Speeches and Writings.* Vol. 7. Oxford: Clio, 2006. Print. The Clio Montessori Ser. Pages 21-28.
[195] Montessori, Maria. *The Absorbent Mind.* Trans. Claude A. Claremont. Vol. 1. Oxford: Clio, 2004. Print. The Clio Montessori Ser. Pages 182-188, 202-222.
[196] Ibid. Pages 202-222.

freedom within natural limits starting on the first day of school. Examples of firmly ingrained ideals within the Casa's culture include respect for personal space as well as respect for the work of others. These aspects of the Casa's culture are reinforced and internalized not though rewards and punishments but through the consistent use of positive phrasing, natural consequences, Grace and Courtesy, peaceful conflict resolution, and the acquisition of normalization.[197] Even before normalization has been achieved, the conditions of the environment itself prepare the child for the spontaneous development of internal and external peace. Beginning on the first day of the Casa,[198] the mixed-age group of children naturally fosters and reinforces the values of patience, kindness, helpfulness, and empathy. Older children who assist younger peers develop positive social skills and experience a boost in self-esteem. Younger children in turn have older peers as friends and advocates. A young child may also be more willing to accept help from a slightly older peer than an adult because the older child, who is more experienced than the younger child, is still close enough in age to his younger peer to understand what level of assistance his classmate requires. These spontaneous interactions among students of various ages lay the foundation for engaging in positive, multi-age interactions that are omnipresent in the world outside the Casa. By maintaining a mixed-age group in the Primary prepared environment, children are free to develop their social skills in a manner that better reflects the outside world than artificially compartmentalized single-age groups.[199]

---

[197] Montessori, Maria. *The Child, Society, and the World: Unpublished Speeches and Writings*. Vol. 7. Oxford: Clio, 2006. Print. The Clio Montessori Ser. Pages 16-19.

[198] A newly opened Montessori Casa may have only three year olds during its first year of operation and add new three year olds to the Casa each subsequent year until a mixed-age group is achieved. This is acceptable as the Casa will eventually have the correct balance of three, four, five, and six year old students to support optimal individual and social development.

Besides mixed-age groups, activities in the environment such as "Walking on The Line" further promote social cohesion through their design. "Walking on The Line" refers to a series of fun, age-appropriate rhythm and equilibrium (balance) games that are typically performed on an outline of an ellipse taped or painted on the floor. This shape is called "The Line." Before using The Line, students must first learn how to stand on The Line, make space by stretching their arms out horizontally to ensure they are not crowding others, and turn to walk. Learning how to exercise enough control to make space and turn to walk in the same direction fosters social cohesion without resorting to lectures and other ineffective moralistic means of conveying to young children about how to get along with one another.[200] If children do not make enough space before turning to walk, everyone will feel crowded. Also, no one can walk until everyone is facing the same direction. When students spontaneously work together to achieve a common goal, such as being able to use The Line for an activity, positive social traits begin to develop and strengthen naturally as a foundation for peace.[201]

While it is important for children to learn how to share The Line when Walking on The Line in the context of a group activity, it is equally important for students to internalize respect for the individual work of others. Learning how to respect the work of others is enforced not through making a list of classroom rules and expectations but through Grace and Courtesy lessons designed to protect a student at work as well as strict adherence to the rules established by the Three Part Work Cycle of choosing work, using work, and putting finished work away in its original condition for the next person to use. Grace and Courtesy lessons that establish and protect personal space include "How to Walk around a Work

---

[199] Montessori, Maria. *The Absorbent Mind.* Trans. Claude A. Claremont. Vol. 1. Oxford: Clio, 2004. Print. The Clio Montessori Ser. Pages 205-208.
[200] Ibid. Pages 175-177, 190.
[201] Ibid. Pages 204-205.

Rug," "How to Observe Someone's Work," "How to Tell if Someone is Working," "What to Say if Someone is Standing Too Close to Your Work," "What to Say if Someone Touches Your Work without Your Permission," and any other lessons about how a student can deliver the Three Part Message to verbally defend himself against peers who violate his personal space. When the guide gives children the means to establish and protect personal space and individual work through her Grace and Courtesy lessons, she helps create a safe, peaceful environment where students are able to work without intrusion or disruption during the uninterrupted three hour work period.

Outside of formal Grace and Courtesy lessons, the guide consistently provides verbal points of interest as needed to remind students to effectively enact the Three Part Work Cycle of choosing work, using work, and putting work away in its proper place in its original condition. While the guide is careful to intervene as little as possible to foster concentration and self-sufficiency, she makes certain that students put finished work away in its proper place in its original condition so that it is ready for the next child's use. If a capable child puts a material away sloppily, the guide has him put the material away correctly. She may say, "Let's make sure this is ready for the next person to use." When a child puts the materials away properly, whether prompted by the guide or not, he is fostering social cohesion by showing respect for his fellow students who have the reasonable expectation that all available materials in the Casa are ready for spontaneous, independent use. Maintaining this respect for the materials, the environment, and peers by keeping manipulatives clean and putting them in their proper place creates an atmosphere[202] where concentration upon freely chosen, well-maintained materials leads

---

[202] Montessori, Maria. *Creative Development in the Child.* Ed. Rukmini Ramachandran. Vol. 1. Chennai: Kalakshetra, 2007. Print. Pages 52-63, 163-166.

to internal and external peace through normalization.[203]

Through consistent Grace and Courtesy lessons and strict adherence to the Three Part Work Cycle within the prepared environment, the guide is able to effectively protect and defend every individual child's personal space as well as his freely chosen, constructive work. Under these positive, pro-social conditions that respect both the individual and the class as a whole, concentration upon freely chosen work can develop as an essential prerequisite to normalization. Once normalization is achieved, social cohesion, the ultimate manifestation of external peace among young children, becomes possible.[204] Following the acquisition of social cohesion within a Casa, students naturally regard their peers as a united community that constantly strives to embody the virtues made possible through normalization.[205] These virtues, among them empathy, respect, kindness, and hospitality, are not only a basis for social cohesion in the Casa but for the world as a whole.[206] Peace established in the Casa through normalization and social cohesion lays a vital foundation for peace in the outside world, an essential prerequisite to universal, harmonious human relations.[207]

---

[203] Montessori, Maria. *The Absorbent Mind.* Trans. Claude A. Claremont. Vol. 1. Oxford: Clio, 2004. Print. The Clio Montessori Ser. Pages 188, 198, 202-203.
[204] Ibid. Pages 212-216.
[205] Ibid. Pages 212-222.
[206] Ibid. Pages 218-222.
[207] Ibid. Pages 219, 222.

Part III

Peace in Practice

Cultivating Peace

Peace is a state of being that is internalized through normalization, the process in which a young child abandons all negative behaviors in exchange for positive behaviors due to concentration upon freely chosen, developmentally appropriate, hands-on work in the Montessori Primary prepared environment.[208] As an internal quality, peace cannot be induced by any external means.[209] Since children under the age of six or seven are concrete sensorial learners rather than rational abstract thinkers,[210] virtues and morality cannot be acquired through fairy tales, myths, fables, empathy training, or lectures.[211] [212] Only the awakening of normalization through the use of practical, concrete, freely chosen work can create internal peace within a young child as a precursor to external peace.[213]

While virtues and morality cannot be taught to First Plane children due to their level of cognitive development,[214] pro-social

---

[208] Montessori, Maria. *The Absorbent Mind*. Trans. Claude A. Claremont. Vol. 1. Oxford: Clio, 2004. Print. The Clio Montessori Ser. Pages 182-188.

[209] Montessori, Maria. *Education for a New World*. Vol. 5. Oxford: Clio, 2005. Print. The Clio Montessori Ser. Pages 60-66.

[210] Montessori, Maria. *The Absorbent Mind*. Trans. Claude A. Claremont. Vol. 1. Oxford: Clio, 2004. Print. The Clio Montessori Ser. Pages 181-191.

[211] Ibid. Pages 180-191.

[212] Montessori, Maria. *The 1946 London Lectures*. Ed. Annette Haines. Vol. 17. Amsterdam: Montessori-Pierson, 2012. Print. The Montessori Ser. Pages 207-217.

[213] Montessori, Maria. *The Absorbent Mind*. Trans. Claude A. Claremont. Vol. 1. Oxford: Clio, 2004. Print. The Clio Montessori Ser. Pages 182-191, 197-214.

behavior modeled through Grace and Courtesy lessons gives young students an effective means of learning, practicing, and applying social skills pertaining to good manners, common classroom procedures, and peaceful conflict resolution. These lessons, combined with developmentally appropriate mixed-age groups, positive phrasing, freedom within natural limits, natural consequences, and the virtues spontaneously acquired through normalization, help create and maintain a peaceful environment within the Casa that serves as a foundation for peace in the wider world.[215]

In addition to the aforementioned prerequisites to peace and social cohesion within the Primary prepared environment, there are many opportunities for students in the Casa to cultivate internal and external peace daily throughout the year with the help of the guide and eventually independently. Several open-ended examples of peace cultivation within the Casa are described in this section under various subheadings for parent and teacher reference.

Geography

Geography, an essential component of Montessori Primary education, encompasses the study of earth's physical geographical features as well as learning about the universal nature of all cultures and individuals. Everyone on earth, regardless of where they live, needs air, water, food, shelter, and love. These universal needs of mankind may be explored in simple picture books or packets of pictures organized by continent that show loving families from around the world caring for their children, providing them with the necessities of life. Once universalities are established, cultural differences regarding human necessities may be explored in an age-appropriate, politically neutral manner. For

---

[214] Ibid. Page 190.
[215] Ibid. Pages 182-191, 202-213.

example, while everyone on earth needs to eat, the particular types of foods humans consume depend largely upon their surrounding physical and cultural environment. A guide may explain differences in diet by showing photographs, telling factual oral stories, and reading picture books to small groups of students about what kinds of foods grow in certain places. Temperate climates, for instance, produce a different range of foods than those found in tropical climates. These types of lessons combine both physical and cultural geography in a factual, non-biased manner that expands young children's understanding of the wider world. For further sensorial exploration, the guide or a guest may also occasionally introduce foods from other places and cultures for students to sample during snack or lunchtime. Following the introduction of a new food, the guide can give basic history lessons to small groups of students about the food's origin, thereby creating a holistic presentation that includes history, geography, botany, biology, and cultural studies to expand the child's knowledge of the world beyond the Casa.

In addition to reading picture books and giving oral presentations to small groups of students, the guide fosters geography studies through the introduction of several individual presentations including "Puzzle Maps." Puzzle Maps, which consist of knobbed puzzle pieces of earth's continents, countries, and states or provinces, provide children with a concrete way to explore our world as a precursor to formal geography studies introduced during the students' elementary years. Although a child can use a Puzzle Map like any other puzzle, these puzzles serve a special purpose in the prepared environment as a catalyst for holistic studies including art appreciation, art history, music appreciation, music history, and other cultural studies. These related geography lessons may be introduced following hands-on experience with the Puzzle Maps in isolation. An example of an age-appropriate cultural geography lesson could be a basic introduction to the history and culture of Impressionist art. Over the course of several days, the guide may introduce examples of Impressionist art and artists in her Casa to an individual child or small group of children with the help of a specific Puzzle Map, photographs, postcards, reproductions of fine art, and other visual aids to enhance appreciation of art from a different era and culture. To draw a connection between Impressionism and geography, the guide may bring out the Puzzle Map of Europe during one or several of her small group presentations and isolate the puzzle piece of France on the rug where the students are gathered as a tangible, visual aid to her lessons about the origins of Impressionist art and its cultural influences.[216] While relating a brief history of Impressionism, the guide can bring her story back to the universality of art by saying something like, "Art has always been important to people all over the world. Although Impressionist art originated far away a long time ago and influenced other cultures, we can still enjoy looking at it today. Some artists living today are inspired by Impressionism when creating original artwork, even though the Impressionist movement took place many years ago." Using the Puzzle Maps and other visual aids in conjunction with age-appropriate oral history presentations helps cultivate global awareness in young children without resorting to lectures or treading upon controversial political issues. Instead of internalizing divisive politics and prejudices, children in the Casa concretely participate in universal human experiences such as art appreciation through the guide's cognitively appropriate, factual lessons that incorporate both the past and present to help lay the foundation for a more peaceful future.

While Montessori guides strive to be politically neutral and unbiased, sometimes changes in the world outside the Casa cannot help entering the prepared environment. A common example of a

---

[216] "Impressionism." *Britannica School.* Encyclopædia Britannica, Inc., 2015. Web. 01 Jan. 2015.
<http://library.eb.com/levels/referencecenter/article/42220#284620.toc>.

political geographical change is when a country alters its borders. When a country changes its political boundaries, the Puzzle Maps are rendered inaccurate. If this happens during the school year before the guide has the opportunity to order a new Puzzle Map, she may introduce "Control Maps" made of paper which show accurate borders. To prevent treading on contentious political topics while still being honest with her students, the guide may gather the children to a rug and say something like, "Our Puzzle Map of (Continent Name) is no longer accurate, so we'll need to use these Control Maps for reference until we can order a new Puzzle Map." If the children question why this is the case, the guide gives a generic, politically neutral answer such as, "Sometimes borders change. We can still use the Puzzle Map of (Continent Name), but remember that the paper Control Map is more accurate." If the students continue to press for more information after hearing the guide's explanation, and the reason for the border change is not an appropriate topic for young children, the guide may say, "Those are really good questions to ask your families at home." The guide then dismisses the group and the day continues as usual. By leaving controversial explanations about border changes in the hands of the children's parents, the guide refrains from inadvertently instilling prejudices in her students while simultaneously respecting their families' beliefs. This policy helps create good social relationships between parents and the guide for a harmonious atmosphere both inside and outside the Casa.

In addition to Puzzle Maps, geography in the Casa is further explored through a set of materials called "Geography Folders" or "Picture Folders." Captioned pictures organized by continent into separate Geography Folders allow children to see glimpses of the world, its peoples, landmarks, buildings, flora, fauna, and geographic features including biomes such as deserts, oceans, tropical rainforests, and coral reefs. Pictures in the Geography Folders, which may include international postcards, travel photographs, and magazine clippings, provide a catalyst for spontaneous or guided discussions about cultures and places. There is one Geography Folder for each continent on earth including Antarctica as well as one Picture Folder for each Land and Water Formation studied in the Casa such as lakes, islands, peninsulas, and gulfs. While the external appearance of Geography Folders may vary by Casa, each folder in a given prepared environment follows a uniform style for ease of independent student use. For organizational purposes, many Casas make Geography Folders from plain manila envelopes labeled with a drawing or photograph of the continent or land and water formation represented. The Geography Folder for South America, for example, should have a photograph or drawing of South America on the front of the envelope either in one of the corners or in the center. All other Geography Folders should be labeled in the same manner for consistency. Between eight and fifteen pictures should be in each folder at all times for student exploration. Geography Folder pictures are rotated occasionally to maintain student interest and encourage repeated use.

A child who has had a lesson in the Geography Folders may choose to look at the captioned pictures from one folder at a time when interested during his uninterrupted three hour work period for leisure and reading practice. Any picture in a Geography Folder can also be used by the guide as a visual aid for an individual or small group presentation about a particular culture, festival, or landmark depicted in the chosen photograph. Geography Folder pictures can also be used as a starting point to Facilitated Conversations between a guide and an individual child or small group of students to promote language development and expand students' knowledge of the world. To lead a Facilitated Conversation with a single student, the guide chooses a picture from one of the Geography Folders, isolates it in front of the child on a table or rug, and then asks him a general, open-ended question such as, "What do you see in this picture?" How the guide continues her open-ended Facilitated Conversation depends upon the individual child's response to her general question about the photograph. If the picture is of a young child riding a bicycle, the student may say that he has a bicycle too, just like the one in the picture! Once the child has drawn a connection between the picture and himself, the guide may emphasize the universal nature of the activity depicted in the photograph by saying something like, "Yes, the girl in this picture is riding a bicycle. People ride bicycles in many parts of the world. Let's see where this picture is from." The guide may then flip the picture over to reveal its caption. If the child is literate, the guide invites him to read what it says. If the child cannot yet read, the guide reads the caption aloud as in, "This caption says, 'Beijing, China.' That's where this picture was taken." After reading the caption, the guide turns the photograph face-up again so the child can see it. Depending on the child's level of interest, the guide can create a more detailed geographic connection by inviting him to take out the Puzzle Map of Asia to locate the puzzle piece representing China. The guide may then place the puzzle piece of China next to the picture to draw a concrete connection between the two objects. How the lesson continues will depend heavily upon the child's cognitive development, level of interest, previous experiences with geography, and any spontaneous comments he makes about the subject. When a lull develops in the discussion, the guide may conclude the Facilitated Conversation by saying, "Thank you for having a conversation with me about this photograph. I am going to do some other work now. What would you like to do next?" If the child wants to continue to look at Geography Folder pictures independently, he is free to do so. The child may also invite a friend to have a conversation with him about pictures in the Geography Folder if he desires. There is also the possibility that the child may be inspired to work with the corresponding Puzzle Map after putting the Geography Folder materials away in their proper place in the Casa. If there are books about geography in the

Reading Corner, the child may want to take a look at them. Cultural activities in the art section may also be available for the child's exploration. And of course, the child may be finished with geography for the present time and choose different work entirely. The beauty of the uninterrupted three hour work period is its flexibility and open-endedness that allows children to continue to explore introduced topics for as long or as little as desired. Like all other studies in the Montessori Primary classroom, geography is integrated within the Casa's holistic environment, available for independent student exploration at the moment of interest in lieu of an adult-imposed schedule. By treating geography in the same manner as other subjects in the Casa, the study of humanity and cultures becomes a natural, integral, and integrated part of the child's life that lays a foundation for positive human relations both locally and internationally, an essential prerequisite to universal, lasting peace.[217]

Art Appreciation and Art History

While Puzzle Maps and Geography Folders are excellent, concrete, hands-on activities that put children in touch with the world outside the Casa, they are only the beginning of a Montessori student's exposure to local and international culture in the Primary prepared environment. In addition to using Puzzle Maps as a visual aid for oral art history presentations about different styles of art and individual artists, the guide incorporates art appreciation into the holistic framework of the Casa by placing reproductions of diverse art representing various eras, movements, cultures, and styles from around the world at the children's eye level throughout the classroom to foster awareness of the universal

---

[217] Montessori, Maria. *The Child, Society, and the World: Unpublished Speeches and Writings*. Vol. 7. Oxford: Clio, 2006. Print. The Clio Montessori Ser. Pages 111-112.

nature of art. These reproductions, which should include artwork from every inhabited continent, can encompass every time period from prehistoric cave paintings to modern art of the twenty-first century. More than mere decoration, these examples of human creation throughout the ages provide children with an all-inclusive experience of culture in addition to serving as a catalyst for thoughtful discussions about individual works of art, the techniques used to produce them, their histories, the lives of the artists, and the cultures that shaped the artists' creations. Art in the Casa is occasionally rotated to further foster art appreciation by maximizing student exposure to the wonder of art as an expression of culture throughout the ages.

As vast, open-ended subjects, art appreciation and art history can be introduced using a variety of techniques appropriate to young, concrete sensorial learners both individually and in small groups. "Facilitated Conversations" between the guide and an individual child or small groups of children about a particular work of art displayed in the Casa help students improve their verbal communication skills and provide a constructive outlet for observation and commentary. During the course of a Facilitated Conversation with an individual student, the guide may subtly incorporate elements of art history by showing the child the artwork's caption which provides the title and artist's name. If the child is literate, the guide may ask him to read the caption aloud. Otherwise, the guide may read the caption to the student. Besides fostering reading practice, reading the artwork's corresponding caption prepares the student for other labeling activities in the Casa and eventually independent research in elementary school. Once the caption is read either by the literate child or the guide, the guide may ask the student a more specific question such as, "Why do you suppose Hokusai called his print, 'Boats in Moonlight?'" The guide respectfully listens to the student's response to gage how to reply. Depending on the child's answer, the guide may provide additional information about the work such as, "Yes, those are boats sailing under the light of the moon. We can see the moon right up here in the corner of the composition. I wonder how many boats are depicted. Let's count them!" The guide and child may then count the boats in the print and make additional observations. While discussing the composition, the guide may interject historical information such as the technique used by the artist and the setting of the image. If the child is interested, the guide may invite him to look at a classroom map or take out the Puzzle Map of Asia to find Japan, the country where Hokusai's "Boats in Moonlight" was printed using woodblocks. Otherwise, the guide may gracefully end the Facilitated Conversation by saying, "Thank you for having a conversation with me. What would you like to do next?" The child may then continue his geography explorations independently or choose other work. Either way, art history, art appreciation, and culture are readily available to the student due to the prepared environment's setup and freedom of work choice that permit independent exploration at the moment of interest rather than during an adult-imposed schedule. The freedom to appreciate art and art history at will allows children to experience the beauty and culture of art as holistic, integrated components of the Casa rather than culture as a mere subject to be learned and later forgotten. When cultural activities that explore and celebrate the universal nature of humanity are treated holistically, they become a vital part of the children's experiences in the Casa. These activities lay a solid foundation for global understanding as a precursor to lasting peace in the world beyond the classroom and its immediate surrounding culture.[218]

Music Appreciation and Music History

Just like art appreciation, music appreciation helps expand a child's global awareness of the universal human need to listen to

---

[218] Ibid.

and produce music. Besides singing songs to children on a daily basis, the guide introduces instrumental music from a variety of cultures and genres on CDs for children to listen to individually and in small groups. Sometime after listening to a particular instrumental piece, the guide may create a small group presentation around the familiar tune that supports music appreciation and a basic understanding of music history. For example, after the students in the guide's group listen to "Für Elise" by Ludwig van Beethoven, the guide may invite two students in the group to bring the Puzzle Map of Europe to the rug and remove the puzzle piece representing Germany to show the students where Beethoven was born. Once the connection between the composer and his birthplace is concretely established by the Puzzle Map piece, the guide may begin to tell a simple, age-appropriate story about Beethoven and his composition, "Für Elise." During her presentation, the guide may explain that "Für Elise" is the German way to say "For Elise," meaning that Beethoven likely dedicated his song to someone named Elise. The guide can connect the composition to the present day by saying something like, "Even though Beethoven wrote the piece we just listened to a long time ago for someone named 'Elise,' we can all enjoy listening to 'Für Elise' today because Beethoven wrote his music down on paper for everyone to read." To further expand the lesson's relevance to her young students, the guide may make a connection between Beethoven's compositions and the compositions that children in the prepared environment can make using the Casa's set of "Movable Bells" by saying, "People living today can compose their own music just like Beethoven did. When people write their compositions down on paper using correct music notation, everyone can appreciate their music forever, just like we can listen to Beethoven's music today. The Bells in our Casa are a good way to start composing original music." By connecting music history to the present day, music appreciation becomes accessible to young learners as a precursor to more advanced music studies in the future and understanding the innate human need for music.

Music appreciation in the Casa extends beyond studying the lives and music of famous composers from various eras and cultures. While there are no separate music teachers in Montessori education as the trained Montessori guide is responsible for every child's education in all subject areas, children's family members who play a musical instrument may occasionally be invited to the Casa to give a short performance. If the guide or her assistant is musically inclined, she may also play an instrument for the children on occasion. Witnessing live music performances whether from the guide or guests is important for young children to help them internalize music as an integrated part of life that is within every individual's reach. Keep in mind that in accordance with the Montessori philosophy of freedom of work choice, students may choose whether or not to attend a musical performance and are free to come and go throughout the presentation as long as their movements are unobtrusive. As children gain more self-control with age and experience, the guide may introduce Grace and Courtesy lessons about how to attend a musical performance or concert and how to be a member of an audience.[219] In the meantime, listening to a musical performance is treated like any other presentation in the Casa in alignment with the cognitive development and natural behaviors of First Plane children.

In the absence of musical instruments, the human voice can be used to express the universal human need for music. Singing and rhythm games such as clapping specific patterns are performed daily with the children starting on the first day of school to continually foster music appreciation throughout the year. Through daily exposure to music from various eras and cultures through both guided and independent activities, children are immersed in an environment that celebrates the universal language

---

[219] Montessori, Maria. *The Discovery of the Child*. Trans. Mary A. Johnstone. Chennai: Kalakshetra, 2006. Print. Pages 78-79, 118.

of music which transcends all eras, cultures, and politics to promote global understanding as a foundation for peace in the Casa and in the world.[220]

Picture Cards and Three Part Cards

Picture Cards

Beyond art and music history, the universality of mankind can be further explored in the Casa through individual Language presentations including "Picture Cards" and "Three Part Cards." Picture Cards, which strongly resemble unlabeled flashcards, are used to introduce vocabulary in the Casa in a clear manner that appeals to the First Plane child's unlimited capacity for language acquisition.[221] To provide a sense of classification, Picture Cards are organized by topic into small decks of no more than ten cards

---

[220] Montessori, Maria. *Creative Development in the Child.* Ed. Rukmini Ramachandran. Vol. 1. Chennai: Kalakshetra, 2007. Print. Pages 196-198.
[221] Montessori, Maria. *The Absorbent Mind.* Trans. Claude A. Claremont. Vol. 1. Oxford: Clio, 2004. Print. The Clio Montessori Ser. Page 159.

each. Topics may be general such as "musical instruments" or specific such as "musical instruments of the percussion family."

Three Part Cards

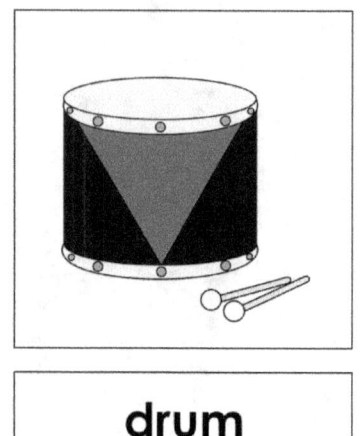

Whether a topic is general or specific, every set of Picture Cards has a corresponding set of Three Part Cards. Three Part Cards, an extension of Picture Cards for literate students, are composed of three parts: unlabeled Picture Cards, Typed Labels, and Control Cards which are labeled Picture Cards. These Three Part Card sets are introduced to older, literate children in the Casa following experience with the corresponding, unlabeled Picture Card sets to foster reading practice.

Since no vocabulary is too difficult for a child under six or seven years of age to learn due to his sensitive period for language,[222] Picture Cards and their corresponding Three Part Cards can cover a variety of topics including gemstone identification, popular car models, famous international landmarks, music composers, types of musical instruments in the woodwind family, art of the 19th century, and so forth. Picture Card sets vary among Casas based

---

[222] Ibid. Pages 100-104, 109, 159-160.

upon the guide's observations of student needs and interests. As there are numerous general and specific topics that may be explored through Picture Cards,[223] Picture Card sets are often created by the guide or her assistant specifically for her prepared environment rather than purchased commercially to help satisfy each young child's insatiable thirst for vocabulary acquisition and to cover topics that may not be available for purchase. To avoid overwhelming students and to maintain interest, Picture Card sets are rotated throughout the year. A culturally competent guide is sure to include Picture Card sets in her Casa that expand her student's knowledge of various subjects beyond the confines of his classroom and surrounding culture. Picture Card sets that may be created to foster global awareness include famous composers of various eras, architectural wonders of the world, natural landmarks arranged by continent, and dwellings from around the world. When creating a Picture Card set, the guide is careful not to subconsciously instill prejudices in her students by offering limiting images of other cultures. In a Picture Card set of famous composers, for example, a certain degree of diversity should be illustrated within the set rather than including only European composers from the classical era to help prevent students from internalizing that only certain types of people can compose music. If appropriate, the guide may also create a Picture Card set of international, modern-day princesses if she has students who are interested in fairy tale princesses to help dispel misconceptions and show what real princesses look like in the twenty-first century. If this or any other Picture Card set topic is too controversial in the surrounding culture, the guide may simply omit questionable cards or create a comparable Picture Card set that is not offensive. When creating Picture Card sets and lessons for her class, the guide is careful to balance global awareness with the beliefs of her

---

[223] Montessori, Maria. *Creative Development in the Child*. Ed. Rukmini Ramachandran. Vol. 1. Chennai: Kalakshetra, 2007. Print. Pages 213-216.

local community to help maintain positive social relationships with her students' families while simultaneously expanding children's knowledge of the world beyond their immediate surroundings to foster understanding and ultimately world peace.

Stories and Music

Geography lessons, art appreciation, art history, music appreciation, music history, Facilitated Conversations, Picture Cards, Three Part Cards, and other individual and small group presentations integrated within the prepared environment's three hour uninterrupted work period are only some of the techniques that can be used to introduce culture in the Casa in an engaging, age-appropriate manner for First Plane learners. In addition to these independent and guided exercises, culture can be introduced beginning on the first day of school simply through exposure to carefully selected stories and music. From day one in the Montessori Casa, a variety of age-appropriate, reality-based fiction and non-fiction picture books are read to students and available for independent reading and viewing in the Reading Corner. While there is no set "Story Time" in the Casa as this would violate student freedom of choice within the three hour uninterrupted work period, the guide is prepared to read at least one fact-based book to interested students per day. A "fact-based" or "reality-based" book in the Primary Casa refers to a story that is believable, accurate, and realistic. Animals in reality-based literature behave like animals in the real world. They do not speak, wear clothes, or otherwise act as substitutes for human characters. Likewise, human children in fact-based books exhibit the natural behaviors of human children. Their explorations and adventures are age-appropriate and realistic but do not show negative behavior in a positive light. Moralistic, fanciful, and symbolic stories such as *Aesop's Fables* and fairy tales are not suitable for children under the age of six or seven due to their abstract nature.[224] Furthermore, normalized First Plane children naturally reject fanciful tales when offered realistic alternatives.[225] Virtues and proper behavior are not instilled through reality-based literature.[226] Instead, these qualities are naturally acquired through normalization[227] as well as Grace and Courtesy.[228] For more information about the purposes and implementation of Grace and Courtesy in the Casa, refer to *Part II: Social Relations*.

Just as important as the provision of a variety of reality-based books in the Casa is the appropriateness of their content for young, impressionable children. At the Primary level, all stories are believable, accurate, and free of political or other bias. Care is taken to avoid presenting books which may subconsciously instill prejudice. Political and other sensitive topics of the past and present are inappropriate for young children and are therefore not presented in the Primary prepared environment. Stories in the Casa may never be used to present an agenda or otherwise propagandize students. Literature in the Casa is not meant to teach children life lessons or virtues; rather, stories are told in the prepared environment to promote "Total Reading." In Montessori Primary education, Total Reading is defined as the capacity to analyze and synthesize the written communication of others through reading comprehension, interpretation of emotional content, and appreciation of individual style. All three essential

---

[224] Montessori, Maria. *The 1946 London Lectures*. Ed. Annette Haines. Vol. 17. Amsterdam: Montessori-Pierson, 2012. Print. The Montessori Ser. Pages 187-192.

[225] Ibid. Pages 188-189.

[226] Montessori, Maria. *The 1913 Rome Lectures*. Ed. Susan Feez. Vol. 18. Amsterdam: Montessori-Pierson, 2013. Print. The Montessori Ser. Pages 259-260.

[227] Montessori, Maria. *Education for a New World*. Vol. 5. Oxford: Clio, 2005. Print. The Clio Montessori Ser. Pages 61-66.

[228] Montessori, Maria. *The Secret of Childhood*. Trans. Barbara B. Carter. Hyderabad: Orient Longman, 2006. Print. Pages 132-135.

elements of Total Reading are introduced and reinforced through the carefully selected literature made available to students in the Primary prepared environment.

Following the criteria for appropriate First Plane books to support the acquisition of Total Reading is a difficult task that requires scrutiny and extremely high standards for literary and artistic quality as well as rooting out books that may subconsciously influence students to adopt negative attitudes toward particular people or cultures. The best way to support understanding of the universal nature of mankind in the Casa through literature is to avoid books that blatantly support or force the idea of tolerance through the use of tokenism. Instead, the guide selects stories that feature believable, well-rounded characters. Books appropriate for children under six or seven years of age do not make an issue out of diversity. The protagonist in a reality-based story should be relevant to any child as demonstrated through the character's activities, feelings, and interests. In essence, the characters in First Plane literature should be universally appealing everymen, or in this case, "everychildren," who are accessible to all students regardless of background. One way to ensure student exposure to the universal nature of mankind is to choose books written by a variety of authors with a wide range of experiences and cultural backgrounds that add to the authenticities of the stories they tell. By selecting literature for the Casa that does not single out diverse characters as somehow "other" or "different," the guide creates an atmosphere of understanding among her students that does not resort to moralizing messages about getting along with one another. This immersion approach to culture through literature, rather than arbitrary unit lessons that artificially force differences to the forefront, provides children with a strong foundation for respecting every individual whether he lives here or elsewhere, an absolutely essential prerequisite to external peace in both the Casa and eventually around the world.[229]

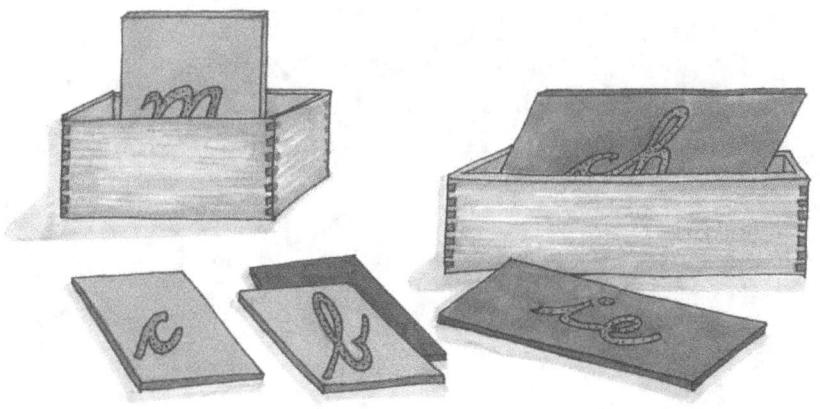

Sandpaper Letters

In addition to fostering Total Reading through constant exposure to diverse, high-quality, reality-based literature and sequential Language manipulatives that aid in the development of literacy, the Montessori guide also creates an environment conducive to "Authorship." Authorship, a uniquely human achievement, is the ability to convey original ideas through writing. The Primary guide supports the acquisition of Authorship by constantly exposing students to rich vocabulary and a variety of hands-on experiences in every subject area that appeal to the First Plane child's sensitive period for language. Literacy preparation manipulatives and exercises, such as the "Sandpaper Letters" and "Movable Alphabet," provide the foundation for children to transcribe their thoughts with ease.

---

[229] Montessori, Maria. *The Advanced Montessori Method II.* Vol. 13. Oxford: Clio, 2006. Print. The Clio Montessori Ser. Pages 174, 178-179, 197-202.

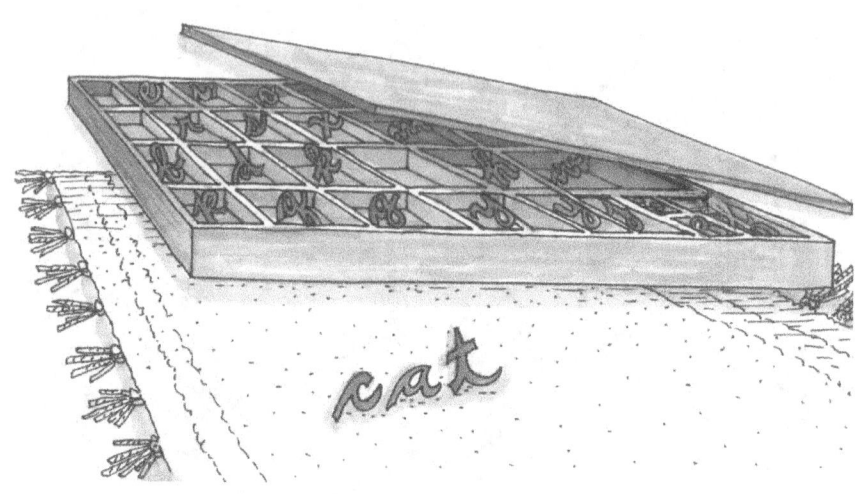

Movable Alphabet

When children first begin to write, they are encouraged to write about something personally meaningful, such as a family pet or their favorite Sensorial exercise. Placing emphasis upon the child's original writing rather than expecting him to copy work from dictation or by rote memorization gives students confidence in their own work. Proper guidance combined with encouragement and a positive attitude toward the young child's original written work positively influences future literary capabilities.[230] Elementary students with a solid foundation in Authorship can research any topic of interest without external guidance. Instead of merely rewording his findings, the Second Plane child, ages six through twelve, draws conclusions based upon his research and records his discoveries in a way which is truly original and meaningful.[231] Besides its academic applications, Authorship

---

[230] Montessori, Maria. *Creative Development in the Child*. Ed. Rukmini Ramachandran. Vol. 2. Chennai: Kalakshetra, 2007. Print. Pages 116-126, 197-224, 276-284.

[231] Montessori, Maria. *The Advanced Montessori Method II*. Vol. 13. Oxford: Clio, 2006. Print. The Clio Montessori Ser. Pages 200-202.

allows students in both the First and Second Planes to engage in creative writing for both practical use and emotional satisfaction. Creative writing, which refers to the child's original written compositions rather than copying from dictation, provides students with a constructive outlet for the imagination. The ability to write original compositions can lead to the creation of simple fiction and non-fiction works which can fill a need in children who feel their stories are not being represented in mainstream literature.[232] Instead of being limited to the stories the guide reads in the Casa, a child who has achieved Authorship has the power to create his own work of literature that reflects his thoughts, ideas, and feelings more accurately than someone else's narrative. The capacity to create an original story thereby validates the child's experiences even if the wider culture does not have books that reflect his knowledge and culture.

While creative writing through Authorship is an important developmental task, writing in the Casa is not confined to poetry, fiction, and non-fiction compositions. In addition to writing original stories and poems, children in the Casa may also write notes to one another in class during the three hour uninterrupted work period to practice writing as a form of silent communication. Learning how to write a note is a vital component of Grace and Courtesy in many cultures whether the note is an invitation, a thank you note, a business letter, a formal letter, or a friendly letter to a family member or friend. When students practice this cultural skill in the prepared environment, they become prepared for writing as a means of positive silent communication and diplomacy for peaceful interactions in the Casa and beyond.

Like literature and creative writing, music in the Casa opens the door to understanding the universal nature of humanity. All

---

[232] Horning, Kathleen T. "Children's Books by and about People of Color Published in the United States." *Cooperative Children's Book Center*. The University of Wisconsin- Madison, 19 June 2014. Web. 12 Jan. 2015. <http://ccbc.education.wisc.edu/books/pcstats.asp>.

cultures have music.[233] Exploration of this universal need of the human race begins on the child's first day of school starting with singing. Just as there is no set "Story Time" in the Casa, there is no pre-determined "Music Time" where students must cease their activities to participate in a music exercise. Instead, the guide is prepared to sing at least one song per day to students who are interested. When a guide sings to a small group of students, children are free to join in when ready. At first, the guide may find herself singing solo, especially when introducing a new song. Eventually, after several repetitions from the guide, children may gradually accompany her although singing is never a requirement. If a child wants to simply listen to the guide while his classmates sing along, no one will force him to sing with everyone else out of respect for his level of confidence and current interests.

When choosing songs for the Casa, the guide uses similar criteria as selecting literature. Songs in the Casa should be relevant to the child and preferably reality-based. The guide may also select music written specifically for Montessori Casas[234] or compose original songs if she is musically inclined. She may also be aware of popular reality-based children's songs from her Montessori training. Regardless of the guide's selection, it is essential to remember that songs in the Primary prepared environment are sung to foster music appreciation as well as satisfy the universal human need for music, not to push an agenda, influence behavior, or otherwise propagandize students. If the guide would like to introduce culture through songs in an unbiased, non-political manner, she may present appropriate children's songs that originate from other cultures or sing in other languages. Since children under the age of six or seven learn foreign languages best

---

[233] Montessori, Maria. *The Absorbent Mind*. Trans. Claude A. Claremont. Vol. 1. Oxford: Clio, 2004. Print. The Clio Montessori Ser. Pages 108-109.
[234] Jones, Sanford. *Youth Opera International: Reach for the Joy of Music!* Youth Opera International. Web. 6 Jan. 2015.
<http://youthoperaintl.com/index.html>.

through total immersion due to their sensitive period for language,[235] it is not necessary for a foreign song to be withheld from the class simply because it is in an unfamiliar tongue. Like any other song, the guide sings the new foreign language song several times and invites the children to join in when ready. In the case of a song in a foreign language, the guide may sing the song a few times with small groups of students and then create follow-up music appreciation lessons about the song's origin, where it was written, and the meaning of the lyrics. As with any music appreciation lesson, the guide may use photographs and the Puzzle Maps as visual aids during her follow-up presentations to expose children to culture in a manner accessible to young, concrete, sensorial learners. Introducing songs from other cultures and languages using the exact same technique as learning any other song exemplifies the global language of music as a foundation for understanding cultural universalities to set the stage for world peace.[236]

Botany

While botany may not seem related to peace education on the surface, a botany activity such as "Flower Arranging" is a peaceful, meditative exercise in the Casa that fosters the development of the aesthetic sense as well as social cohesion. When a child in the prepared environment prepares a bouquet for the Casa using the Flower Arranging materials, he is not only satisfying his own emotional needs but making the room more beautiful for his classmates as well. Social skills are often required when placing the finished flower arrangement in the room as the child may want to ask a peer if he would like a bouquet on his

---

[235] Montessori, Maria. *The Absorbent Mind*. Trans. Claude A. Claremont. Vol. 1. Oxford: Clio, 2004. Print. The Clio Montessori Ser. Pages 98-115, 158-160.
[236] Ibid. Pages 108-109.

work table. Besides Flower Arranging, botany studies and plant care foster respect for the environment as plants must be handled gently to prevent damage. Working with real plants and flowers prepares students to handle and care for other living things such as classroom pets. This care for living things can then be extended to care for others, not only members of the child's immediate social group, but care and concern for humanity as a whole to promote universal peace.[237]

Collective Exercises

Although most activities in the Casa are designed for individual use in accordance with a First Plane child's cognitive development,[238] there are a few exercises in the prepared environment which require collaboration in order to best support the exercise's function and optimal outcome. These select group activities usually include two to five students. Group activities that require ten or more students are rare.[239] Regardless of whether a small group activity has two or ten students, cooperation is required to achieve a positive result. A common example of activities that work best with small groups of students rather than individually are the "Collective Exercises" in Mathematics.

---

[237] Ibid. Pages 200-201, 210-213.

[238] Montessori, Maria. *The Secret of Childhood*. Trans. Barbara B. Carter. Hyderabad: Orient Longman, 2006. Print. Pages 146-148.

[239] Examples of group exercises which require ten or more students in the Casa include select Group Memory Games and the Memory Game of Numbers. These activities are not directly related to the topic of peace education and are therefore not described further in *The Peace Table*.

Collective Exercise: Addition

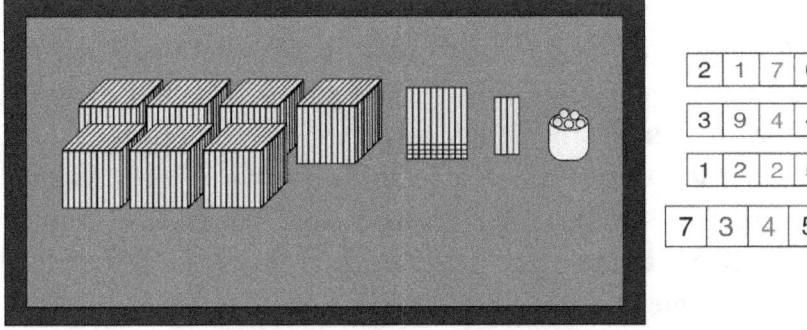

Dynamic Addition, Final Layout

Each of the Collective Exercises focuses on one of the four operations of mathematics: addition, subtraction, multiplication, or division. "Collective Exercise: Addition," the first Collective Exercise presented,[240] involves combining two to four addends to achieve a sum. To illustrate the additive process in a manner that makes sense to young, concrete, sensorial learners, quantities are represented by beads and number cards. If there are three children playing, there will be three numbers to add such as "2176," "3944," and "1225."[241] Each child in the group is responsible for one of the aforementioned numbers in the addition problem which he must represent with the corresponding quantity beads and number cards. After gathering his materials, he joins the other children at the rug where the quantities will be combined on a tray and sorted into their correct decimal system categories of ones, tens, hundreds, and thousands. Following counting, the number cards are aligned vertically on the right-hand side of the rug in a manner similar to the appearance of an addition problem on paper.

---

[240] The first Collective Exercise is "Static Addition," meaning that no numbers need to be carried to achieve the sum. Following mastery of Static Addition, "Collective Exercise: Dynamic Addition" is immediately introduced.

[241] In the Casa, commas are not used for numbers over "1,000" until the child gains more experience and is less likely to be confused by the comma's significance.

Once the quantities are placed on the rug in their proper locations, the children work together to figure out the sum of their addition problem by counting the unit beads first, followed by the tens, hundreds, and thousands. If any category adds up to more than ten, the child in charge of counting that category must exchange beads at "the store," an area in the Casa where bead counting materials are stored. Ten unit beads, for example, must be exchanged for a single bar of ten beads, which is added to the pile of tens that the children have already gathered. Likewise, as the counting continues, it may become necessary for ten bars of ten beads each to be exchanged for one square of one hundred beads and ten squares of one hundred beads each to be exchanged for one cube of one thousand beads. When all the beads are counted and appropriate decimal system exchanges have been made, the children discover the sum, which is then recorded with the corresponding number cards. At this point, it is not necessary for the students to record their findings on paper as the emphasis of all the Collective Exercises is mastery of the process of the four operations of mathematics rather than memorizing and recording the answers to various equations.[242] In addition to concretely practicing the processes of each of the four mathematical operations for academic reasons, social skills are reinforced and strengthened through the Collective Exercises' cooperative design. Rather than competing against other students when studying mathematics, children working with the Collective Exercises assist one another so that everyone in the Casa can eventually achieve independent academic success. Pride in one's own achievements and happiness for the successes of others, two of the universal traits of normalization,[243] are allowed to flourish in the prepared

---

[242] Memorizing essential math facts as well as recording and solving original equations in the four operations of mathematics is explored later in the Casa following extensive hands-on experience with the process of each mathematical operation through the Collective Exercises and other relevant activities including The Stamp Game, the individual version of the Collective Exercises.

environment's atmosphere where cooperation rather than competition leads to success and the wonder of discovery.[244] Natural, spontaneous cooperation exhibited in the Collective Exercises and other activities throughout the Casa help strengthen positive, constructive interactions with peers as a foundation for cooperation in the world outside the classroom for the establishment of lasting peace.[245]

The Silence Game and its History

Silence is not the normal state of the Casa. Most of the time, the sounds of manipulatives being used, happy conversation, and group activities such as singing or Collective Exercises fill the air of the prepared environment. Despite the busy hum of the Children's House, there is one whole-class activity in which the children joyfully create and maintain total silence. This favorite, counterintuitive exercise is known as "The Silence Game."[246]

Like many of the exercises in the Casa, The Silence Game was not born out of educational fads or an attempt to make children behave in a certain manner; rather, The Silence Game was one of the many accidental discoveries made by Dr. Maria Montessori pertaining to the universal needs and interests of three through six year old children. One day, when showing a silent four month old baby to a group of First Plane children, Dr. Montessori jokingly commented that it would be impossible for the students to be as

[243] Montessori, Maria. *The Absorbent Mind*. Trans. Claude A. Claremont. Vol. 1. Oxford: Clio, 2004. Print. The Clio Montessori Ser. Pages 183-184, 206-213.
[244] Montessori, Maria. *Dr. Montessori's Own Handbook*. Mineola: Dover Publications, 2005. Print. Pages 74-79.
[245] Montessori, Maria. *The Child, Society, and the World: Unpublished Speeches and Writings*. Vol. 7. Oxford: Clio, 2006. Print. The Clio Montessori Ser. Pages 22-25.
[246] Montessori, Maria. *Creative Development in the Child*. Ed. Rukmini Ramachandran. Vol. 1. Chennai: Kalakshetra, 2007. Print. Pages 76-83.

silent and still as the baby in her arms. To her surprise, the children suddenly became quiet and still.[247] This was the first time Dr. Montessori observed young students becoming silent without external compulsion or reward. Later, Dr. Montessori conducted a hearing test with her entire class by having the children wait silently in the adjacent room while she called each child individually by name in a whisper. Thinking this would be a strenuous task for such young children, Dr. Montessori was prepared to reward each silent child with a piece of candy for coming when called. To her surprise, the children refused the external reward for creating and maintaining silence. The students enjoyed the activity so much, they asked Montessori when they could play the game again! Based upon the children's enthusiastic reactions during both the incident with the silent baby and the hearing test, Dr. Montessori made the popular Silence Game an integral feature of the Primary prepared environment. Following several repetitions of The Silence Game with her class, Dr. Montessori discovered that not only did children enjoy the activity but their awareness of the environment grew to the point where students moved carefully and courteously throughout the classroom so as not to carelessly bump into furniture, make too much noise, or otherwise disturb their fellow classmates. This spontaneous student attention to careful movements and consideration for others born from the calm, meditative nature of The Silence Game led to the acquisition of internal discipline and positive human relationships.[248] Like normalization, The Silence Game has the capacity to cultivate a state of peace both in the individual child and the Casa as a whole, making it an essential component in every Primary prepared environment.[249]

---

[247] Montessori, Maria. *The Child, Society, and the World: Unpublished Speeches and Writings*. Vol. 7. Oxford: Clio, 2006. Print. The Clio Montessori Ser. Pages 50-58.

[248] Montessori, Maria. *Creative Development in the Child*. Ed. Rukmini Ramachandran. Vol. 1. Chennai: Kalakshetra, 2007. Print. Pages 76-83.

Important Considerations for The Silence Game

Like all other group activities in the Casa, The Silence Game is an invitation rather than an imposition. Although The Silence Game requires the participation of the entire class simultaneously, a rarity within the Casa, the guide must still gage her students' willingness to participate through careful observation of the current atmosphere of the prepared environment. If the class is energetic, it is not an appropriate time to initiate The Silence Game. The guide should instead lead groups of students in gross motor activities such as square dancing or marching with musical instruments like a parade, exercises which are in alignment with the current energy level of the room. It is essential that the guide follow the children's energy and current interests when leading activities so that students will want to participate in The Silence Game voluntarily. By not introducing The Silence Game on a noisy day, the guide respects and protects the purpose of the exercise. The purpose of The Silence Game is to help students reach their highest level of coordination for their holistic development and well-being. As an exercise designed for the betterment of the students, The Silence Game must never be used to enforce quiet behavior for the guide's convenience. Misuse of The Silence Game constitutes a form of external control rather than the culmination of the children's accomplishments in voluntary, internally motivated motor control. It is only when The Silence Game is used correctly that true internal peace can be cultivated as a precursor to external peace and universal serenity.[250]

A calm atmosphere in the Casa is not the only consideration the guide needs to keep in mind before initiating The Silence

---

[249] Montessori, Maria. *Dr. Montessori's Own Handbook*. Mineola: Dover Publications, 2005. Print. Pages 74-79.

[250] Montessori, Maria. *Creative Development in the Child*. Ed. Rukmini Ramachandran. Vol. 1. Chennai: Kalakshetra, 2007. Print. Pages 76-83.

Game. It is also essential that all students in the room are experienced enough to play The Silence Game successfully. As a game that requires tremendous self-control and coordination of movement, particularly the inhibition of almost all voluntary movements, The Silence Game cannot be introduced with a new class of students who have not yet mastered basic levels of self-control. Developing enough self-control to participate in The Silence Game requires practice through several preliminary exercises that prepare students to successfully and joyfully partake in The Silence Game with the entire class. These preliminary exercises are described in the following paragraphs.

Preliminaries to The Silence Game

While The Silence Game cannot be immediately introduced to a Casa due to its difficulty and requirement of cooperation among all students in the class, preparations or preliminaries to The Silence Game can be played on a daily basis beginning on the first day of school with students of all ages. Activities that help children exercise and improve upon gross and fine motor coordination as well as self-control vary by Casa and culture. Familiar traditional childhood games like "Simon Says," "Duck, Duck, Goose," and "Red Light, Green Light," can be excellent starting points to prepare students in the Casa for The Silence Game. These group games and similar activities require a combination of synchronized coordinated movements as well as the inhibition of movements at specified intervals to help young children gain mastery over their own bodies enabling them to move gracefully and purposefully as they work and play in the Casa and wider world. Mastery over gross and fine motor movements, typically practiced through repeated use of Practical Life activities including coordination games and exercises, is an essential prerequisite to all future social, emotional, and academic work in the Casa and beyond.[251]

In addition to traditional childhood games, the guide may introduce a fun Silence Game prerequisite activity called "Move and Still." To play Move and Still, the guide begins by setting up child-sized chairs for her group. Alternatively, if there are older children who will be playing alongside their younger peers, the guide may invite them to help her set up the chairs in a semi-circle or row in front of a single chair where the guide will sit. Once the chairs are arranged, the guide invites a small group of students one at a time to play a game with her. After the children are seated, the guide sits on the chair in front of the students and thanks them for joining her group. Before continuing, the guide makes sure the children have good posture, which is essential for the game. If the students are not sitting with good posture, the guide models correct posture and makes verbal points of interest as necessary such as, "Put your feet flat on the floor and place your hands on your knees like me. Let's sit up straight and tall!" As soon as the children are seated correctly, the guide gives a series of commands that alternate between movement and stillness. For the first command, the guide may say, "Wiggle your fingers." The children and guide then wiggle their fingers until the guide says, "Now keep your fingers still." After giving the stillness command, the guide stops moving her fingers and waits for the children to stop wiggling their fingers. Following a few seconds of stillness, the guide gives a new movement command such as, "Tap your toes." The movement command is then followed by the appropriate stillness command, "Now keep your toes still." After giving several movement and stillness commands, the guide has the children close their eyes and sit in silence. When the children begin to fidget or look tense, the guide ends the activity by reciting a familiar poem or singing a quiet familiar song to conclude Move and Still on a calm note. When finished, the guide thanks the

---

[251] Ibid. Pages 52-59, 159, 182-183, 192-199.

children for playing with her and then dismisses students individually in the usual fashion. If there are older, more experienced students in the group, the guide may have the children put their chairs back before choosing other work. Following dismissal, the guide notes the lesson in her records, making note of which students can perform the exercise well and which students need more practice. It is essential to note that games which contrast movements versus stillness are simply games. They are played for the children's entertainment and to assist them in building awareness of their own body movements to help them refine their gross and fine motor coordination for future activities, not for any ulterior motives or the guide's convenience.

After playing Move and Still a few times with small groups of children, the guide can add commentary to the game to further build student awareness of what it means to move versus being still and silent. Instead of reciting a poem or singing a song after the period of silence at the end of Move and Still, the guide can say something like, "When we were all very still and quiet, we made silence. We all made silence together." Once children understand what is meant by "silence," the guide can introduce additional extensions to the original Move and Still game at a later time. The guide then dismisses her students individually in the usual manner.

When children understand what is meant by "silence" due to their experiences with Move and Still and the guide's accompanying commentary, the guide can help children become aware of sounds in the environment by asking them what they heard during their silence. To do this, the guide has the children make silence following Move and Still as usual. At the end of the silence, the guide may ask, "What sounds did you hear when we all made silence?" The children may then call out their answers one at a time giving examples such as, "the sound of the clock ticking," "the sound of other students working nearby," or "birds singing." If none of the children have anything to contribute, that is perfectly acceptable as well. Now that the guide has asked students about the sounds they heard during silence, the children may listen more closely the next time they play Move and Still. Asking children to describe what they heard during silence is a good auditory exercise that helps students realize that sounds are created outside of their own activities, an excellent way to naturally and sensorially promote awareness of the wider world and its various occurrences.

Another variation of Move and Still exercises a child's ability to localize sounds as well as his control and coordination of movement. To play, the guide invites a group of students to sit on chairs as usual. This time, the guide has the children close their eyes and tells them to point to where she is in the room when she makes a sound. After explaining the game, the guide silently walks away from the group and makes a small noise such as dropping a pencil on the floor or clapping her hands once somewhere in the Casa. The children then point to the location of the noise with their eyes closed. While they are pointing, the guide tells them to open their eyes to see if they were correct. After confirming the guide's location, the children close their eyes again so the guide can move somewhere else and make a small noise. Each time the guide makes a noise and the children close their eyes again, the guide waits slightly longer between each noise and silence to help the students refine their patience while simultaneously exercising control and coordination of movement as well as auditory perception. At the end of the exercise, the guide returns to the children, thanks them for playing with her, and then dismisses the group in the usual fashion.

Besides Move and Still, children can explore movement versus stillness through an activity called "Fifteen Seconds of Silence." To play, the guide invites a group of students one at a time in the usual manner to sit on chairs or on the floor. When everyone is seated, the guide says, "Let's close our eyes and sit absolutely still." If the children have been playing movement games including Move and Still, the process of being still and silent is already familiar. In fact, the guide may reinforce the meaning of silence by saying, "Let's all make silence," instead of giving a detailed explanation of what to do. Once the silence begins, the guide looks at her watch or a clock with a second hand to accurately judge the passage of time. If the students become restless before fifteen seconds have passed, the guide gracefully ends the activity by inviting the children to open their eyes. She then concludes by telling the children how long they made silence as in, "We just made ten seconds of silence." Depending upon the energy of the children and the guide's observations of the individual students in her group, she may end the activity by reciting a poem, singing a quiet song, or simply help students transition to their individual work if they are growing too restless to continue the current exercise. Following the calm conclusion of the activity, the guide dismisses the group as usual. If the children did not achieve fifteen seconds of silence, the game can always be played another day. No child is ever singled out for his inability to create silence for a specified period of time. As the students become more proficient at achieving fifteen seconds of silence, the guide gradually increases the interval of silence to twenty seconds, then thirty seconds, and eventually an entire minute or more. To introduce and reinforce knowledge of time as a prerequisite for learning how to tell time, the guide may begin Fifteen Seconds of Silence or any of its variations by saying, "Let's see what fifteen seconds feels like." Fifteen Seconds of Silence then proceeds as usual albeit with the preceding verbal suggestion that children can now physically experience the meaning of fifteen seconds. At the end of Fifteen Seconds of Silence, the guide can further reinforce the meaning of time progression by stating the usual conclusion, "We just made fifteen seconds of silence." In another variation of Fifteen Seconds of Silence, the guide can ask the children what they heard during the silence. This variation of the game can also be played outdoors in nice weather to enhance auditory awareness of the sounds of nature such as birds chirping or wind rustling through the trees. Regardless of how the guide presents Fifteen

Seconds of Silence and its variations, the most important aspect of gameplay is that the guide takes the lead from her students so the exercise remains enjoyable rather than tedious or punitive. Once again, creating silence in a group setting is for the children's holistic development and enjoyment, not to enforce calm behavior or for the guide's convenience.

In addition to small group activities such as Fifteen Seconds of Silence, gross motor preparations for The Silence Game also include all Walking on the Line activities. The Line, usually an outline of an ellipse taped or painted on the floor, gives children the opportunity to practice rhythm and equilibrium (balance) in a manner that also fosters social cohesion. Before doing any rhythm or equilibrium activities on The Line, children must first learn how to stand still on The Line. After learning how to stand on The Line, students must learn how to make personal space by stretching their arms out to their sides. If a child's arm or arms touch another person when stretched out, the child must figure out how to move so that his arms and hands no longer touch anyone else. Once children know how to make space, they must turn to walk before actually walking on The Line. Unless every child using The Line is facing the same direction, no one can walk on The Line without creating a collision. Surprisingly, deciding to all face the same direction based upon group consensus rarely requires adult intervention.[252] Most of the time, children figure out how to turn in the same direction without the guide telling them which way to turn,[253] especially if the guide gives the verbal point of interest, "If you see someone's eyes, you can turn the other way." Learning how to turn in the same direction to walk on The Line with minimal adult assistance supports and strengthens social cohesion as well as respect for personal space as precursors to

---

[252] Montessori, Maria. *The Absorbent Mind*. Trans. Claude A. Claremont. Vol. 1. Oxford: Clio, 2004. Print. The Clio Montessori Ser. Page 204.
[253] Ibid.

peace in the Casa and beyond.[254]

Once children know how to stand on The Line, make space, and turn to walk, the guide can begin to introduce various rhythm and equilibrium activities that support gross motor coordination and balance. The Walking on the Line activities introduced and practiced on a daily basis in the Casa help children gain control of their bodies so they can navigate throughout their world safely, efficiently, and courteously.[255] By strengthening their coordination in an enjoyable manner, children also strengthen their characters as mastery of the body through hands-on work leads to concentration and eventually normalization,[256] the process in which a young child spontaneously abandons all negative behaviors in exchange for positive behaviors.[257] The physical, intellectual, and emotional strength built and practiced through movement activities including traditional childhood games, Move and Still, Fifteen Seconds of Silence, and Walking on the Line prepares students for the ultimate control and coordination of movement exercised through The Silence Game as a prerequisite for peaceful coexistence in the Casa and outside world.[258]

The Silence Game

After all movement preliminaries have been practiced, and children in the Casa exhibit a reasonable degree of concentration, coordination of movement, and self-control, as well as the ability to follow directions, The Silence Game can finally be introduced.

---

[254] Ibid.

[255] Montessori, Maria. *Creative Development in the Child.* Ed. Rukmini Ramachandran. Vol. 1. Chennai: Kalakshetra, 2007. Print. Pages 64-67.

[256] Ibid. Pages 52-75, 154-159, 176, 178-183.

[257] Montessori, Maria. *The Absorbent Mind.* Trans. Claude A. Claremont. Vol. 1. Oxford: Clio, 2004. Print. The Clio Montessori Ser. Pages 182-191.

[258] Montessori, Maria. *Creative Development in the Child.* Ed. Rukmini Ramachandran. Vol. 1. Chennai: Kalakshetra, 2007. Print. Pages 64-83.

Before initiating The Silence Game, the guide observes her classroom to ensure the proper environmental conditions are in order. The first observation the guide makes is of the atmosphere of the Casa. If there is a high level of calm and self-control in the room, The Silence Game may be an appropriate activity to introduce. As always, the guide may never use The Silence Game to subdue a rowdy classroom as this is an abuse of the activity's purpose as a means of helping an already calm class further refine and perfect their well-developed coordination and concentration skills for the children's holistic development. Besides the energy level of the Casa, the guide also observes her students' current activities. If one or more students are deeply engrossed in their work, The Silence Game cannot be played as it would interrupt their concentration.[259] [260] In addition to these considerations, the guide must also be aware of the time it will take to play The Silence Game. Since The Silence Game can be quite lengthy depending upon the children's level of interest and concentration, the guide must ensure there will be enough time to complete the activity without rushing into a transition period such as lunch or pick-up time immediately following the exercise. In addition to time constraints, the guide must also be sure that everyone in the room will be able to participate. If a parent is visiting the class as an observer, it is not a good time to play The Silence Game as the activity requires the participation of everyone in the room, including any adult assistants in the Casa. Moreover, playing The Silence Game in front of a parent visitor may give an incorrect impression of Montessori education as The Silence Game is not a regular occurrence in the classroom. As a final consideration, the guide must keep in mind a situation where a single student may not want to participate. In this rare circumstance, the guide may have

---

[259] Ibid. Pages 78, 82-83.

[260] Montessori, Maria. *The Child, Society, and the World: Unpublished Speeches and Writings*. Vol. 7. Oxford: Clio, 2006. Print. The Clio Montessori Ser. Pages 55, 57.

the assistant discreetly take the child to work or play outside during the duration of The Silence Game so that his movements do not disrupt his fellow classmates.

Once the guide has observed that the Casa meets the proper conditions for The Silence Game, she gets the children's attention. How she does this depends upon her class and her students' prior experiences. If this is the children's first time playing The Silence Game, the guide may make a calm, quiet, general announcement in the room or invite children individually to play a game. Later in the year, once the children are more experienced, the guide can initiate The Silence Game using a silent signal such as writing the word "Silence" on a chalkboard instead of making a verbal announcement.

After announcing The Silence Game, either verbally or with a silent signal, the guide invites the children to find a place in the room where they can sit or lie down comfortably without making any sounds. If the children have previous experience with The Silence Game, the silent signal may be enough to prompt them to find a place to make silence without any verbal explanations from the guide. A child may sit on the floor or on a chair as he chooses as long as his choice allows him to be comfortably still and silent for the duration of the activity. As soon as the children are settled, the guide explains any additional game rules if necessary, and then either stands or sits on a chair while she waits in one area of the room without making a sound. Following a long period of silence, the guide whispers the name of one of the children who is perfectly still and silent. The child who hears his name whispered should stand up as carefully and silently as possible and walk over to the guide. After reaching the guide, the child sits down in front of her and waits while the game continues. Following another long pause, the guide calls a second child to her location in a faint whisper. Once the child who is called walks over to the guide and sits down, another period of silence occurs until the guide whispers the next child's name. One by one, the children who are making silence are called over to the guide until all participating students, and the adult assistant if present, are called. If a child does not hear his name when called, the guide moves on to the next child and returns to the other student later. If a child is not making silence, the guide waits to call him until he regains composure. In the event that several children fidget and the game is losing its silent quality, the guide concludes the activity by making a general quiet announcement such as, "Anyone who is still sitting can walk over to me as quietly as possible."[261] This group conclusion is not a punitive practice but a sensible, graceful way to end The Silence Game without singling anyone out if students are growing restless.

Once all the children are gathered near the guide following The Silence Game, the guide may conclude the exercise by reciting a familiar poem or singing a short, quiet song as a gentle transition to the students' next work choices. This part of The Silence Game is optional and based upon the guide's observations of her group. Regardless of whether or not the guide recites a poem or sings a song in transition, the guide ends the exercise by saying, "Thank you for playing with me." After thanking the children for their participation, the guide dismisses the students individually in the usual fashion. Life in the Casa then continues as usual.

While not a regular exercise in the Casa, The Silence Game provides students with the opportunity to exercise the ultimate mastery of their self-control and coordination of movement in preparation for a highly developed academic and social life.[262] The Silence Game's inherently calming, meditative nature, reliance upon social cohesion, and ability to make children more attentive to the sounds around them helps students elevate their relationships with peers and the environment. Children who play The Silence

---

[261] The use of the word "can" instead of "may" is intentional as the Montessori guide is affirming what the children are able to do rather than giving permission.
[262] Montessori, Maria. *The Child, Society, and the World: Unpublished Speeches and Writings.* Vol. 7. Oxford: Clio, 2006. Print. The Clio Montessori Ser. Pages 51-57.

Game become more aware of their movements and seek to navigate their surrounding environment with great care so as not to damage materials or disturb others at work. In addition to fostering graceful movements, The Silence Game heightens a child's awareness of others which supports spontaneous pro-social behavior in the Casa as a precursor to peaceful relationships with others in the world outside the classroom for the betterment of humanity as a whole.[263]

Peace in the Home

Parents and the Montessori guide form a vital partnership in every child's holistic education that encompasses his physical, intellectual, and emotional development. More than a mere system of schooling, Montessori is a lifestyle that must be adopted by the student's family to help bring the child to his fullest potential in every area both socially and academically. For every child, education begins in the home long before he is old enough to consciously make sense of the world around him.[264] Starting at birth through six or seven years of age, children internalize their surrounding environment in totality without filters due to the power of the absorbent mind. Driven by their sensitive periods for order, movement, refinement of sensory perception, and language, young children instinctively seek out activities in their environments which appeal to the five senses of vision, hearing, smell, touch, and taste. The combination of the absorbent mind and sensitive periods allows First Plane children without reasoning minds to effortlessly learn from their environments as they are too young to be taught at a rational level.[265] The problematic aspect of

---

[263] Montessori, Maria. *Creative Development in the Child.* Ed. Rukmini Ramachandran. Vol. 1. Chennai: Kalakshetra, 2007. Print. Pages 80-83.
[264] Montessori, Maria. *The Secret of Childhood.* Trans. Barbara B. Carter. Hyderabad: Orient Longman, 2006. Print. Pages 33-41.

effortless learning through the absorbent mind is that without reason or conscience as a guide, children under the age of six or seven absorb everything in the world around them and internalize what they perceive through the five senses, both positive and negative.[266]   For this reason, parents must be mindful when creating a home environment for their young, impressionable children.   If the home is disorderly and chaotic, the child will internalize disorder and chaos which will subsequently become permanently ingrained features of his character if not resolved by the end of the First Plane of development before reaching roughly seven years of age.[267] When something is amiss in the child's environment, collective stage or negative behavior is likely to occur. Usually, various episodes of misbehavior in a young child including tantrums are indicative of an environmental issue that requires correction. In the case of a misbehaving young child, it is the *environment* that requires correction rather than the child[268] as the child cannot disobey the instincts dictated by his sensitive periods for order, movement, sensory perception, and language.[269] Rather than thwarting a child's strong, internal motivation to act upon his environment, it is better to provide age-appropriate, hands-on, constructive activities that appeal to his five senses in order to foster concentration as an essential prerequisite to normalization, the process in which a child spontaneously

---

[265] Montessori, Maria. *The Absorbent Mind*. Trans. Claude A. Claremont. Vol. 1. Oxford: Clio, 2004. Print. The Clio Montessori Ser. Pages 17-19, 22-26, 46-47, 52, 55-61, 65-69, 72-88, 90-93, 114-115, 130-131, 139-141, 145-150, 152-156, 170, 177, 190.

[266] Ibid. Pages 178-182.

[267] Montessori, Maria. *Creative Development in the Child*. Ed. Rukmini Ramachandran. Vol. 1. Chennai: Kalakshetra, 2007. Print. Pages 233-234.

[268] Montessori, Maria. *The Child, Society, and the World: Unpublished Speeches and Writings*. Vol. 7. Oxford: Clio, 2006. Print. The Clio Montessori Ser. Pages 75-81.

[269] Montessori, Maria. *The Secret of Childhood*. Trans. Barbara B. Carter. Hyderabad: Orient Longman, 2006. Print. Pages 33-41.

abandons all negative behaviors in exchange for positive behaviors. Normalization is only possible in a prepared environment best suited to the needs and interests of three through six year old children.[270] It is only after normalization has been achieved that internal peace can be acquired as a precursor to external peace.[271] For peace to become truly internalized in a young child as a direct result of normalization, it is imperative that parents and Montessori guides become partners in early childhood education so that children can experience cognitively appropriate, consistent environments at home and school for optimal holistic development.[272] Following are several suggestions for how parents can foster normalization and peace in the home as essential precursors to global peace.

Modeling Grace and Courtesy

Peace in the home begins with the adult who provides a developmentally appropriate environment for their child while simultaneously modeling and exemplifying peaceful, pro-social behavior. To help your child internalize positive behavior and social niceties, always strive to model peaceful, civil conduct both at home and in public. Gently and consistently correct any negative behavior displayed by your child by stating the positive alternative rather than issuing criticisms or punishments. Use positive phrasing that tells your child what to do rather than what not to do. If your child picks his nose, for example, say, "You can use a tissue for your nose," rather than, "Don't pick your nose!" After showing your child where to find a tissue, have him wash his hands for hygiene. Once the incident is over, allow life to continue

---

[270] Montessori, Maria. *The 1946 London Lectures*. Ed. Annette Haines. Vol. 17. Amsterdam: Montessori-Pierson, 2012. Print. The Montessori Ser. Page 219.
[271] Ibid. Pages 152-157, 218-238.
[272] Ibid. Pages 225-238.

as usual. At a later time, you can introduce a Grace and Courtesy skit on "How to Use a Tissue for Your Nose" to prepare your child to handle future incidents appropriately with minimal or no external guidance.

Just as in the Montessori Casa, you can introduce Grace and Courtesy lessons at home isolated from a behavioral incident to help your child learn and practice good manners, common procedures, and peaceful conflict resolution skills. If you notice your child exhibiting a negative behavior such as not saying, "Excuse me," when someone is in his way, create an applicable Grace and Courtesy lesson using the standard Grace and Courtesy technique of verbally introducing the lesson, modeling the lesson, inviting the child to practice the lesson, summarizing the lesson, and then dismissing the child to do other work. To give a lesson on "What to Do When Someone is in Your Way," you can invite the child's older siblings or other family members to assist you. An older child can stand in the way of a shelf so that you can model saying, "Excuse me," with a person who is actually in the way of something. Alternatively, you can demonstrate the lesson by yourself. Once you have arranged your presentation, invite your child to play with you. Have him sit on the floor while you sit on a stool or stand. Introduce your lesson with a brief verbal summary of the skill you are going to model as in, "I am going to show you what to do when someone is in your way." If you have a family member as an assistant, walk up to the person and say, "Excuse me." The other person should then say, "Certainly," and step aside so you can pass. If you are modeling by yourself, which may not be as effective, walk over to an area of the room and say, "Excuse me," and then wait before passing the imaginary obstruction. Whether you use an assistant or not, return to your child when finished and say, "Now it's your turn. Show me what to do when someone is in your way." If you have a helper, have the child say "Excuse me" to your assistant. If you are presenting the lesson by yourself, have your child practice with you by saying, "Let's practice together!" Following a brief practice period, conclude your lesson with a brief verbal summary as in, "Now you know what to do when someone is in your way." Ask your child what he would like to do next or simply transition to the next activity. Make a mental or written note of the lesson. Remember that one Grace and Courtesy lesson is never enough. Plan to review each Grace and Courtesy lesson several times over the course of a few days or weeks to provide your child additional practice with each presented skill. Refer to *Part II: Social Relations* for additional ideas regarding Grace and Courtesy implementation.

When infractions occur despite Grace and Courtesy lessons and positively phrased points of interest such as, "You can use a tissue for your nose," remember to consistently apply natural consequences rather than punishments. Instead of issuing time-outs when your child misbehaves, distract him with an interesting activity and plan to give an appropriate Grace and Courtesy lesson at a later time. If distraction is not a viable option for resolving the current situation, focus instead upon how the child can make amends or solve the problem. For example, if the child breaks a glass, help him to safely clean up the broken pieces with a broom and dustpan under careful supervision. Once the pieces are safely gathered and disposed of, allow life to continue as usual. At a later time you can give your child a Grace and Courtesy lesson review about how to carry objects carefully. In response to a more serious matter such as hitting or biting, deliver the Three Part Message before offering a distraction. The Three Part Message concisely names the undesired behavior, states your opinion of it, and tells the instigator what you want him to do. An example of a Three Part Message delivered by an adult to a child may sound like, "You hit me! I don't like that! Don't hit me again!" Depending on the situation, you could then walk away from your child to demonstrate that you do not want to play with him when he is aggressive, and return shortly thereafter to distract him with a different activity. Alternatively, you can use positive phrasing to redirect his negative behavior such as saying, "You can use your words to tell me how you feel," or "Hitting is not acceptable! We are going to find a different way to express your feelings." If your child is capable, talk him through the incident to help him learn how to express himself verbally rather than physically. Regardless of how you handle the situation, remember to remain calm and realize that children under six or seven years of age lack a reasoning mind.[273] [274] After the incident has passed, plan to give an applicable Grace and Courtesy lesson to help your child internalize positive behavior. Never forget that Grace and Courtesy lessons can be used to address any undesirable behavior by a child under the age of six or seven rather than resorting to punishments because of the young child's innate desire to adopt the practices, behaviors, and mores of the surrounding culture.[275]

Although it is important to consistently correct inappropriate behavior by using positive phrasing as well as Grace and Courtesy lessons, it is equally essential to never praise your child for behaving properly as this may cause him to rebel rather than internalize good behavior. Instead, when your child behaves himself, act as though nothing is out of the ordinary, even if your child rarely displays the particular positive behavior in question. Over time, the combination of always intervening with positive phrasing for negative behavior and treating positive behavior as an expectation rather than a praiseworthy event should help your child internalize appropriate social graces that can be exercised successfully at home, school, and elsewhere as a precursor to peace and positive social relations everywhere.[276] [277]

---

[273] Ibid. Page 209.

[274] Montessori, Maria. *The Absorbent Mind.* Trans. Claude A. Claremont. Vol. 1. Oxford: Clio, 2004. Print. The Clio Montessori Ser. Page 190.

[275] Ibid. Pages 157, 165-174.

[276] Montessori, Maria. "Some Words of Advice to Teachers, 1924." *The Call of Education* 11.IV (1925). *Montessori Article.* Association Montessori

The Peace Table at Home

While it is important to consistently address misbehavior through gentle verbal points of interest as well as Grace and Courtesy lessons, it is equally important not to force children to apologize for breaking rules or hurting someone either physically or emotionally. Forcing children to say "I'm sorry," is a detrimental practice as it promotes dishonesty and does nothing to resolve the current situation. Instead of expressing a rehearsed, automatic apology every time a conflict arises, it is better for children to learn how to solve their problems through positive communication skills that strengthen diplomacy to help foster positive human relations.[278] To encourage and support peaceful conflict resolution in the home, create a Peace Table where your child, his siblings, and friends can amicably resolve their disputes with limited adult intervention. To make The Peace Table, place a child-sized table in an easily accessible area of your home. Place two child-sized chairs at the table across from each other. Put an object symbolic of peace such as a dove figurine in the middle of the table. The object symbolic of peace will act as an inanimate mediator during a conflict. Whoever is holding the object speaks and the other person listens silently and respectfully. After speaking, the child holding the object hands it to the other person. It is now the other person's turn to speak while the first child listens silently. This simple turn-taking exercise may require your help at first, but the goal is for your child to eventually be able to

Internationale, 2005. Web. 3 June 2011. Page 3.

[277] Montessori, Maria. *The Discovery of the Child*. Trans. Mary A. Johnstone. Chennai: Kalakshetra, 2006. Print. Pages 74-79.

[278] Goertz, Donna B. "Did You Say "Sorry?": Seeing Through Montessori Eyes." *Parenting for a New World* XVI.2 (2008). *AMI/USA News*. Association Montessori Internationale, Apr. 2008. Web. 6 Dec. 2014.
<http://donnabryantgoertz.com/2013/wp-content/uploads/2014/12/AMI-Did-You-Say-Sorry.pdf>.

solve conflicts with his siblings and friends without any adult assistance. When you are initially assisting children at The Peace Table, remember your role as a mediator and adhere to peaceful conflict resolution practices. The Peace Table is a safe place where children can peaceably resolve their disputes with limited adult interference, not a place where judgment is passed by an authority figure such as the parent or teacher. Keep in mind that using The Peace Table to its best advantage requires practice. It may be necessary in the beginning for the adult to intervene in order to help children make progress in their discussion or have them take a break for a while if the issue does not seem to be moving toward a resolution. Always strive to meet the ultimate goal of spontaneous, independent use of The Peace Table as a precursor to diplomacy throughout the child's life as a foundation for peace in the wider world.

Humility and Honesty

Besides modeling Grace and Courtesy and using The Peace Table to amicably resolve disputes, adults in the child's life must also exhibit humility. Humility can begin by being honest if you do not know the answer to your child's question. Instead of offering a fictitious explanation, say, "I don't know. Let's go look that up!" If you believe your child's question cannot be answered in an age-appropriate manner or are otherwise taken by surprise, you can say, "I don't know what to say about that. I'll have to think about what you just asked me." This honest, neutral answer may be sufficient to satisfy your child's curiosity. If not, your response has given you time to think of an age-appropriate answer you can give later after taking time to consider the question.

Although a sensitive topic, in accordance with the Montessori philosophy of adult humility and honesty, presenting Santa Claus, the Tooth Fairy, and other fanciful figures to young children is strongly discouraged.[279] According to Dr. Montessori, it is wrong for adults, including family members, to take advantage of a young child's lack of experience for their own amusement by introducing fanciful figures such as Santa Claus as fact.[280] While presenting fairy tale figures like Santa Claus as factual may seem innocuous, intentionally misleading children erodes the virtues of honesty, trustworthiness, and respect.[281] Propagating falsehoods of this nature whether out of a sense of tradition or adult enjoyment also injures the child's inherent dignity and creates a serious obstacle to his intellectual development.[282] Rather than sparking a child's imagination as is commonly thought,[283] fantasy actually weakens it by obfuscating reality.[284] In order to cultivate the imagination, an essential developmental characteristic, children require hands-on, cognitively appropriate, reality-based experiences that support optimal holistic development.[285] [286] The development of the imagination best occurs in a peaceful prepared environment that exemplifies the virtues of honesty and mutual respect as a precursor for internal and external peace.[287] If the subject of fanciful figures arises in conversation despite adherence to reality-based education, you can interject brief, age-appropriate, historical

---

[279] Montessori, Maria. *The Advanced Montessori Method I*. Vol. 9. Oxford: Clio, 2004. Print. The Clio Montessori Ser. Pages 200, 202-205.

[280] Ibid. Pages 200, 202-203.

[281] Ibid. Page 202.

[282] Ibid. Pages 199-205.

[283] Montessori, Maria. *Creative Development in the Child*. Ed. Rukmini Ramachandran. Vol. 1. Chennai: Kalakshetra, 2007. Print. Page 173.

[284] Montessori, Maria. *The Advanced Montessori Method I*. Vol. 9. Oxford: Clio, 2004. Print. The Clio Montessori Ser. Pages 196-205.

[285] Montessori, Maria. *The Absorbent Mind*. Trans. Claude A. Claremont. Vol. 1. Oxford: Clio, 2004. Print. The Clio Montessori Ser. Pages 160-170.

[286] Montessori, Maria. *To Educate the Human Potential*. Vol. 6. Oxford: Clio, 2003. Print. The Clio Montessori Ser. Pages 8-11.

[287] Montessori, Maria. *The Child in the Family*. Trans. Nancy R. Cirillo. Vol. 8. Oxford: Clio, 2006. Print. The Clio Montessori Ser. Pages 47-62.

information about the mentioned topic instead of ignoring it. For example, if your child mentions Santa Claus, you can tell a brief, age-appropriate, factual story about how the tradition of Santa Claus was based upon St. Nicholas, a real person who lived a long time ago who was known for anonymous gift giving. To help prevent conflict with children who believe in Santa Claus and fairy tales, it may be advisable to tell your child in advance that other children may believe in Santa Claus, the Tooth Fairy, and so forth, so it is better to agree to disagree than to get into an argument. How you decide to handle the introduction of fantasy in your home will depend largely upon your individual circumstances. When making decisions regarding fanciful figures, keep in mind the Montessori philosophy of reality-based education for the preservation of dignity[288] and the development of the intellect[289] in preparation for internal and external peace.

Beyond being truthful at a cognitively appropriate level, humility also requires the adult to constantly model respectful behavior regardless of her audience. This includes occasionally displaying contrition. Simply put, apologize if you are in the wrong even if that means saying, "I'm sorry" to your own child. While telling a child, "Say you're sorry!" promotes dishonesty and can weaken diplomacy,[290] it is appropriate to model being sorry in front of your child if the situation warrants so that he can internalize positive human relationships. Likewise, if your child is in your way, remember to say, "Excuse me." If you accidentally

---

[288] Montessori, Maria. *The Advanced Montessori Method I*. Vol. 9. Oxford: Clio, 2004. Print. The Clio Montessori Ser. Pages 199-205.

[289] Montessori, Maria. *Creative Development in the Child*. Ed. Rukmini Ramachandran. Vol. 1. Chennai: Kalakshetra, 2007. Print. Page 173.

[290] Goertz, Donna B. "Did You Say "Sorry?": Seeing Through Montessori Eyes." *Parenting for a New World* XVI.2 (2008). *AMI/USA News*. Association Montessori Internationale, Apr. 2008. Web. 6 Dec. 2014. <http://donnabryantgoertz.com/2013/wp-content/uploads/2014/12/AMI-Did-You-Say-Sorry.pdf>.

brush past him, say "Excuse me," or, "I'm sorry." Remember to say, "Thank you," when it is appropriate to express gratitude. The only way a child can truly internalize Grace and Courtesy as a precursor to widespread peace is if it is consistently modeled by the adults closest to him[291] and offered universally to all people regardless of age or cultural differences.[292]

Fostering Normalization in the

Prepared Home Environment

Modeling proper behavior and peaceful conflict resolution skills through Grace and Courtesy is not enough to create a peaceful home environment. In order for a young child to attain fully realized peace, he must first be normalized.[293] Normalization, the process in which a child spontaneously abandons all negative behaviors in exchange for positive behaviors, is an essential prerequisite to internal and external peace[294] as well as joyful academic achievement.[295] The acquisition of normalization, a phenomenon unique to children under six or seven years of age,[296] can only be achieved through concentration upon hands-on,

---

[291] Montessori, Maria. *The Discovery of the Child*. Trans. Mary A. Johnstone. Chennai: Kalakshetra, 2006. Print. Pages 120-122.

[292] Montessori, Maria. *The Secret of Childhood*. Trans. Barbara B. Carter. Hyderabad: Orient Longman, 2006. Print. Pages 133-135.

[293] Montessori, Maria. *Education and Peace*. Vol. 10. Amsterdam: Montessori-Pierson, 2008. Print. The Montessori Ser. Pages 30-32, 53-59.

[294] Montessori, Maria. *The Absorbent Mind*. Trans. Claude A. Claremont. Vol. 1. Oxford: Clio, 2004. Print. The Clio Montessori Ser. Pages 182-191, 202-222.

[295] Montessori, Maria. *The 1946 London Lectures*. Ed. Annette Haines. Vol. 17. Amsterdam: Montessori-Pierson, 2012. Print. The Montessori Ser. Pages 216-217.

[296] Montessori, Maria. *Creative Development in the Child*. Ed. Rukmini Ramachandran. Vol. 1. Chennai: Kalakshetra, 2007. Print. Pages 233-234.

developmentally appropriate work that appeals to the sensitive periods for order, movement, refinement of sensory perception, and language.[297] A carefully prepared environment is a vital requirement for the transformation from collective stage[298] to normalization to occur.[299] With the attainment of normalization comes internal and external peace, essential foundations for peace on a global scale.[300]

While a Montessori Primary Casa complete with the entire array of scientifically designed and tested manipulatives, large mixed-age groups for socialization, and the trained Montessori teacher for appropriate guidance provides the optimal setting for the awakening of normalization, there are techniques and practices you can implement at home to help create consistent environments for your child both at home and school. Begin by organizing your children's toys and activities on easily accessible open-shelving. Displaying toys and games on open shelves instead of throwing them into a disorganized toy chest provides a clear sense of order and demonstrates that every item has a proper place. In addition to displaying your child's toys and games in a logical, organized manner on open shelves to promote purposeful use of materials, implement the Three Part Work Cycle of choosing work, using work, and then putting work away in its original condition in its proper place to establish clear expectations that foster personal responsibility and provide consistency between the Casa's prepared environment and the home's prepared environment.

---

[297] Montessori, Maria. *The Secret of Childhood*. Trans. Barbara B. Carter. Hyderabad: Orient Longman, 2006. Print. Pages 33-68, 144-148.

[298] "Collective stage" refers to any deviations or instances of misbehavior present in children who are not yet normalized.

[299] Montessori, Maria. *The 1946 London Lectures*. Ed. Annette Haines. Vol. 17. Amsterdam: Montessori-Pierson, 2012. Print. The Montessori Ser. Pages 212-238.

[300] Montessori, Maria. *Education for a New World*. Vol. 5. Oxford: Clio, 2005. Print. The Clio Montessori Ser. Pages 61-66.

When your child chooses work, or a toy for that matter, have him work at a child-sized table or on rug to define his workspace and to help prevent clutter. As soon as your child is finished working, make sure he puts the toy or manipulative away before selecting a new material. This expectation helps maintain order in your child's mind and work by preventing untidiness which in turn helps foster respect for the rules of Three Part Work Cycle designed to promote harmony in the classroom and home environments.

Just as essential as implementing and consistently enforcing the Three Part Work Cycle is selecting materials and activities that best support your child's holistic development through hands-on learning. When selecting activities for your child, choose high-quality materials such as wooden building blocks rather than plastic substitutes to encourage careful handling, a vital, lifelong skill. Having too many virtually indestructible plastic toys invites careless use rather than careful handling that is promoted by beautifully made, natural, delicate materials.[301] Beautiful, fragile materials such as ceramic bowls, glass cups, and wooden blocks displayed in a visually appealing manner on easily accessible open shelves naturally attract children's attention, which is the first step in establishing a connection between a child and a manipulative. If a manipulative is unpleasant to any of the senses or otherwise bland and uninteresting, a child will not want to concentrate upon it. As concentration is the basis for the acquisition of normalization, the materials in a child's environment must be beautiful, precisely measured, and open-ended to encourage spontaneous and joyful repeated use.[302]

In accordance with the Montessori philosophy of intrinsically motivated activity, foster learning as its own reward by not issuing gold stars or praise for work well done as rewards can be just as

---

[301] Montessori, Maria. *The Advanced Montessori Method I*. Vol. 9. Oxford: Clio, 2004. Print. The Clio Montessori Ser. Pages 232-234.
[302] Ibid. Pages 53-75, 111-132, 232-234.

detrimental as punishments to learning.[303] [304] Instead of offering external motivations, make the child's environment as beautiful and organized as possible in alignment with his sensitive periods for order, movement, sensory perception, and language.   An attractive environment that internally motivates children to act upon it due to their sensitive periods is sufficient to induce concentration without the motivation of external rewards.[305] When a child spontaneously concentrates upon freely chosen, hands-on, cognitively appropriate work without external interference including praise, normalization is able to emerge as an essential prerequisite to internal peace which in turn lays the foundation for external peace in the home, school, and ultimately the world.[306]

While Montessori is not opposed to toys, keep in mind that children usually prefer realistic alternatives if given the choice.[307] When children play, they are actually mimicking adult behavior[308] and have been known to exhibit frustration when their developmentally important explorations are limited to manufactured toys that have limited possibilities for use.[309] A common example of adult mimicry is when children host a pretend tea party with stuffed animals. In the Montessori Casa, children do

---

[303] Montessori, Maria. *The Absorbent Mind*. Trans. Claude A. Claremont. Vol. 1. Oxford: Clio, 2004. Print. The Clio Montessori Ser. Pages 224, 255.

[304] Montessori, Maria. *The 1913 Rome Lectures*. Ed. Susan Feez. Vol. 18. Amsterdam: Montessori-Pierson, 2013. Print. The Montessori Ser. Pages 126-137.

[305] Montessori, Maria. *The Discovery of the Child*. Trans. Mary A. Johnstone. Chennai: Kalakshetra, 2006. Print. Pages 83-84.

[306] Montessori, Maria. *Education and Peace*. Vol. 10. Amsterdam: Montessori-Pierson, 2008. Print. The Montessori Ser. Pages 76-91.

[307] Montessori, Maria. *The Secret of Childhood*. Trans. Barbara B. Carter. Hyderabad: Orient Longman, 2006. Print. Page 128.

[308] Montessori, Maria. *The 1946 London Lectures*. Ed. Annette Haines. Vol. 17. Amsterdam: Montessori-Pierson, 2012. Print. The Montessori Ser. Pages 151-157.

[309] Montessori, Maria. *The Advanced Montessori Method I*. Vol. 9. Oxford: Clio, 2004. Print. The Clio Montessori Ser. Page 234.

not have to settle for a fictitious tea party but instead learn how to perform a real tea ceremony with their friends. Although the adult must handle all parts of the exercise related to the stove and hot water for safety, children are able to participate meaningfully in the majority of the activity. Every aspect of serving tea that is not performed by the adult for safety is the responsibility of the children. This includes everything from inviting their friends to making finger sandwiches to pouring real lukewarm tea. Compare this scenario to that of the pretend tea party. While a pretend tea party with stuffed animals may be mildly amusing, it cannot compete with the joy children receive when using their best manners to host an actual tea party complete with party preparations, tea, homemade treats, and guests.[310] In addition to its enjoyable nature, hosting a simple tea party helps children practice important practical life and social skills pertaining to food preparation, table manners, and the art of conversation, skills that cannot be exercised to their fullest extent during a fictitious tea party with inanimate objects as guests.[311]

Beyond hosting actual tea parties, students in the Casa learn to care for themselves, their classmates, and their environment through various hands-on Practical Life exercises that fulfill young children's need to purposefully act upon their world to learn and grow from it. Practical Life activities including but not limited to dusting, sweeping, polishing, and washing are the starting point for every child's developmental work in the Casa as these tasks provide the most common catalyst for concentration which in turn awakens normalization.[312] You can foster concentration upon freely chosen, Practical Life activities at home just like in the Casa.[313]

[310] Ibid. Pages 232-234.

[311] Montessori, Maria. *The Secret of Childhood*. Trans. Barbara B. Carter. Hyderabad: Orient Longman, 2006. Print. Pages 161-163.

[312] Montessori, Maria. *Creative Development in the Child*. Ed. Rukmini Ramachandran. Vol. 1. Chennai: Kalakshetra, 2007. Print. Pages 180-183.

[313] Montessori, Maria. *The Absorbent Mind*. Trans. Claude A. Claremont. Vol. 1.

Begin by assessing your living space and culture. Since Practical Life exercises are designed to help children improve their gross and fine motor coordination, foster concentration, and adapt to their surrounding culture in accordance with their innate desire to emulate the adults in their lives, there is no official list of Practical Life activities that must be introduced. The Practical Life exercises presented in a given Casa are heavily influenced by the culture in which the classroom resides as well as the guide's observations of individual student needs and interests. Likewise, when preparing activities for your child at home, keep the culture of your household in mind. If you do not have brass figurines or sculptures at home, you probably do not need to show your child how to polish brass as brass polishing is not applicable to the culture of your home. Instead, offer alternative, comparable practical activities that are relevant to your home which allow for the development and refinement of fine motor control. Consider purchasing real child-sized brooms and dustpans for actual use around the house instead of offering your child doll-sized pretend brooms and dustpans to "play house." To further promote concentration, responsibility, and care of the environment, provide potted plants in your home's indoor or outdoor environment for your child to water and wash the leaves. If you have pets, involve your child in age-appropriate tasks such as measuring pet food. For hygiene and functional independence, have either a hand washing station or step stool so your child can access the sink independently to wash his hands. Help combat tantrums by telling your child your plans for the day in the morning rather than simply announcing you are going to the store moments before you plan to leave. Also consider implementing a timer-based time management system to help give your child a small choice in the daily routine to further dissuade tantrums. A few minutes before you intend to go to the store, ask your child if he would like to leave now or in ten

Oxford: Clio, 2004. Print. The Clio Montessori Ser. Page 182.

minutes. If your child says "ten minutes," set a timer for ten minutes and make it clear that when the timer sounds, it is time to leave. You can use this timer system for a variety of situations including when to do chores and when to get dressed. This system gives children a small choice in their lives in preparation for larger decisions they will have to make when they are older. Schedule your time so that small choices your child makes allow for punctuality, a vital, lifelong social skill that shows respect for other people's time. Regardless of which activities you offer your child at home, always be consistent, allow for change, and supervise for safety. In addition to safety concerns, be attentive to your child's level of concentration and interest when doing Practical Life work. If your child is completely uninterested in a particular exercise, offer an alternative activity that still provides developmentally essential experiences related to motor control. When your child becomes completely engrossed in an activity, take care not to disturb him unless absolutely necessary. Breaking a child's concentration upon freely chosen, cognitively appropriate, purposeful work can cause reluctance to voluntarily concentrate in the future which hinders the awakening of normalization.[314] Do not panic if your child becomes so focused upon a material that he repeats the exercise forty or more times in succession. This is normal and to be expected in young children,[315] particularly those under four-and-a-half years of age.[316] Always remember that the purpose of Practical Life activities is to foster spontaneous concentration as an essential prerequisite to normalization. The acquisition of normalization provides the basis for all successful intellectual[317] and social work in the future.[318] When you foster

---

[314] Ibid. Pages 255-256.

[315] Montessori, Maria. *The Secret of Childhood.* Trans. Barbara B. Carter. Hyderabad: Orient Longman, 2006. Print. Pages 124-126.

[316] Montessori, Maria. *The Discovery of the Child.* Trans. Mary A. Johnstone. Chennai: Kalakshetra, 2006. Print. Pages 244-245.

[317] Montessori, Maria. *Creative Development in the Child.* Ed. Rukmini

concentration as a precursor to normalization through naturally appealing, reality-based work, you help lay the foundation for internal peace within your child which can then be transformed into external peace followed by social cohesion. After the acquisition of social cohesion, the ultimate manifestation of external peace and harmony in children under six or seven years of age, peace beyond the confines of the home and classroom becomes possible as a foundation for universal harmony.[319]

Since the acquisition of normalization requires concentration upon cognitively appropriate, reality-based, hands-on work, it is not recommended within the Montessori community that children under the age of six or seven engage in virtual-based technology such as video games, computers, or television viewing.[320] [321] Children under six or seven years of age are intrinsically motivated by their sensitive periods for order, movement, refinement of sensory perception, and language to choose activities that help them exercise and perfect their gross and fine motor control as well as positive communication skills.[322] [323] Pushing buttons on a computer or video game and passively watching television do not

Ramachandran. Vol. 1. Chennai: Kalakshetra, 2007. Print. Pages 206-207, 212.

[318] Montessori, Maria. *The Absorbent Mind*. Trans. Claude A. Claremont. Vol. 1. Oxford: Clio, 2004. Print. The Clio Montessori Ser. Pages 182-190, 197-222, 255.

[319] Ibid. Pages 212-222.

[320] Long, John. "The Technology Screen: A Compilation by Three Authors: Jumpstart Baby." *AMI/USA*. Web. 10 Jan. 2015.
<http://amiusa.wpengine.com/wp-content/uploads/2012/03/amiusa-the-technology-screen.pdf>.

[321] Montanaro, Silvana Q. "The Technology Screen: A Compilation by Three Authors: Television and the Young Child." *AMI/USA*. Web. 10 Jan. 2015.
<http://amiusa.wpengine.com/wp-content/uploads/2012/03/amiusa-the-technology-screen.pdf>.

[322] Montessori, Maria. *The Discovery of the Child*. Trans. Mary A. Johnstone. Chennai: Kalakshetra, 2006. Print. Pages 105-122, 353.

[323] Montessori, Maria. *The Secret of Childhood*. Trans. Barbara B. Carter. Hyderabad: Orient Longman, 2006. Print. Pages 124-148.

provide children with vital developmental skills.[324]   Keep this in mind when pressured to purchase the latest gadgets for your child's alleged development.   Even so-called "educational games" are still virtual-based rather than reality-based and typically do not exercise the child's whole body for the development of gross and fine motor control.[325] [326] Despite mainstream insistence upon immersing children in the most recent technology, remember that the laws of development are universal throughout all cultures and eras. [327] [328] Young children need to exercise their whole bodies and use their hands in order to learn[329] and become normalized,[330] essential developmental experiences often absent in environments overly obsessed with computer proficiency at an early age.[331]   The universal instinct in children under the age of six or seven to improve their control and coordination of movement due to their sensitive periods[332] is as strongly innate in the twenty-first century

[324] Long, John. "The Technology Screen: A Compilation by Three Authors: Jumpstart Baby." *AMI/USA*. Web. 10 Jan. 2015. <http://amiusa.wpengine.com/wp-content/uploads/2012/03/amiusa-the-technology-screen.pdf>.

[325] Ibid.

[326] Montanaro, Silvana Q. "The Technology Screen: A Compilation by Three Authors: Television and the Young Child." *AMI/USA*. Web. 10 Jan. 2015. <http://amiusa.wpengine.com/wp-content/uploads/2012/03/amiusa-the-technology-screen.pdf>.

[327] Montessori, Maria. *What You Should Know about Your Child*. Vol. 4. Amsterdam: Montessori-Pierson, 2008. Print. The Montessori Ser. Pages 47-49.

[328] Montessori, Maria. *The Absorbent Mind*. Trans. Claude A. Claremont. Vol. 1. Oxford: Clio, 2004. Print. The Clio Montessori Ser. Page 185.

[329] Montessori, Maria. *What You Should Know about Your Child*. Vol. 4. Amsterdam: Montessori-Pierson, 2008. Print. The Montessori Ser. Pages 9-11.

[330] Montessori, Maria. *The 1946 London Lectures*. Ed. Annette Haines. Vol. 17. Amsterdam: Montessori-Pierson, 2012. Print. The Montessori Ser. Pages 212-217.

[331] Long, John. "The Technology Screen: A Compilation by Three Authors: Jumpstart Baby." *AMI/USA*. Web. 10 Jan. 2015. <http://amiusa.wpengine.com/wp-content/uploads/2012/03/amiusa-the-technology-screen.pdf>.

as it was in an era before electronics.[333] As for preparedness for the twenty-first century, remember that children today are technology natives.[334] Thanks to the absorbent mind's power of cultural adaptation, children are already being immersed in the latest electronics simply by living in the world around them.[335] Moreover, young children have the rest of their lives to master the technological advances of the current era. In contrast, sensitive periods for gross and fine motor development diminish or disappear as a child ages. Order, movement, and sensory perception begin to fade or disappear completely around four-and-a-half years of age.[336] Language remains an intense motivation through the age of six.[337] In light of the brief, ephemeral nature of the sensitive periods, it is clear that modern technology can wait. The time to provide hands-on experiences for children to act upon their sensitive periods for their holistic development is now.[338] Without activities that promote concentration, normalization is highly unlikely if not impossible.[339] As the foundation for internal

---

[332] Montessori, Maria. *The Secret of Childhood.* Trans. Barbara B. Carter. Hyderabad: Orient Longman, 2006. Print. Pages 206-210.

[333] Montessori, Maria. *The Child, Society, and the World: Unpublished Speeches and Writings.* Vol. 7. Oxford: Clio, 2006. Print. The Clio Montessori Ser. Page 74.

[334] Prensky, Marc. "Digital Natives, Digital Immigrants." *On the Horizon* 9.5 (2001): 1-2. *Marc Prensky.* MBC University Press, Oct. 2001. Web. 12 Jan. 2015. <http://www.marcprensky.com/writing/Prensky%20-%20Digital%20Natives,%20Digital%20Immigrants%20-%20Part1.pdf>.

[335] Montessori, Maria. *The Absorbent Mind.* Trans. Claude A. Claremont. Vol. 1. Oxford: Clio, 2004. Print. The Clio Montessori Ser. Pages 57-61.

[336] Montessori, Maria. *The Discovery of the Child.* Trans. Mary A. Johnstone. Chennai: Kalakshetra, 2006. Print. Pages 244-245.

[337] Montessori, Maria. *The Absorbent Mind.* Trans. Claude A. Claremont. Vol. 1. Oxford: Clio, 2004. Print. The Clio Montessori Ser. Page 159.

[338] Montessori, Maria. *The Advanced Montessori Method I.* Vol. 9. Oxford: Clio, 2004. Print. The Clio Montessori Ser. Pages 62-63.

[339] Montessori, Maria. *The Absorbent Mind.* Trans. Claude A. Claremont. Vol. 1. Oxford: Clio, 2004. Print. The Clio Montessori Ser. Pages 182-188.

and external peace, normalization through hands-on, developmentally appropriate, reality-based materials must be your first priority as a foundation for peace in the home that can be extended to peace in the wider world.[340]

Besides hands-on work with reality-based materials rather than electronics and passive entertainment, fostering strong, positive communication skills is an essential prerequisite for peace. The development of communication begins with the adult. Always speak to your child intelligently using complete sentences and correct grammar so that he can learn sufficient vocabulary to articulate his needs in words. Since children under the age of six or seven possess the sensitive period for language, there is no vocabulary too difficult for a young child to learn.[341] Baby talk and insufficient dialogue with your child do a severe disservice to his development[342] and hinder his ability to use his words to resolve conflicts peaceably.[343] [344] When young children cannot communicate due to underdeveloped language skills, tantrums are likely to occur.[345] To aid language development for creating a peaceful environment, lead your child in purposeful conversations as frequently as possible, taking care not to start a conversation when he is concentrating upon purposeful, hands-on work for his development in other areas. Conversations with your child do not need to be complicated and can cover topics that adults may find mundane. When at the grocery store, for example, you can tell your child something like, "Let's see. I have seven items on our

---

[340] Ibid. Pages 186, 188, 190, 202-204, 209-213, 218-219, 221-222.

[341] Ibid. Pages 100-104, 158-160.

[342] Montessori, Maria. *The 1913 Rome Lectures*. Ed. Susan Feez. Vol. 18. Amsterdam: Montessori-Pierson, 2013. Print. The Montessori Ser. Pages 201, 231-236.

[343] Montessori, Maria. *The 1946 London Lectures*. Ed. Annette Haines. Vol. 17. Amsterdam: Montessori-Pierson, 2012. Print. The Montessori Ser. Pages 58-60.

[344] Montessori, Maria. *The Absorbent Mind*. Trans. Claude A. Claremont. Vol. 1. Oxford: Clio, 2004. Print. The Clio Montessori Ser. Pages 111-115.

[345] Ibid. Pages 111-115.

shopping list that we need to find. The first item on our list is 'whole wheat bread.' Since the bread is in aisle one, we should go there first." While explaining tasks to your child in this manner, make sure to pause occasionally in case your child wants to contribute to the conversation. You can also ask him questions about what you are doing such as, "Where do you suppose they keep the milk in this grocery store?" Keep any questions fun and upbeat rather than constantly quizzing your child as though you are conducting a test. In addition to fostering communication skills through dialogues at home and in public, support a strong family connection by establishing a regular time for all members of the household to eat together as children do in the Casa to promote meaningful conversations and social cohesion. When it comes to conversations, whether at home or elsewhere, take the lead from your child. If he asks questions or makes comments, tailor your conversation to appeal to his current interests when possible. Gently and consistently correct any grammar mistakes, word misuse, and mispronunciations by simply saying the correct word so your child can internalize and apply proper language usage at home and in public.[346] Knowing how to speak correctly and fluently provides a solid foundation for diplomacy at The Peace Table and throughout life as an essential precursor to lasting peace.[347] [348]

In addition to the aforementioned suggestions, ask your child's Primary Montessori guide for additional ideas on how to create a prepared home environment that is consistent with the Casa's prepared environment. Your partnership with your child's trained Montessori guide is essential to support optimal individual, intellectual, and social development.[349]   When you and the

---

[346] Montessori, Maria. *The 1946 London Lectures*. Ed. Annette Haines. Vol. 17. Amsterdam: Montessori-Pierson, 2012. Print. The Montessori Ser. Pages 58-60.

[347] Ibid. Pages 144-150.

[348] Montessori, Maria. *The 1913 Rome Lectures*. Ed. Susan Feez. Vol. 18. Amsterdam: Montessori-Pierson, 2013. Print. The Montessori Ser. Page 201.

[349] Montessori, Maria. *The Secret of Childhood*. Trans. Barbara B. Carter.

Montessori guide work together for your child's benefit, you help lay a solid foundation for the internalization of peace, an essential prerequisite to external peace.[350] External peace in the Casa created by normalization ultimately manifests itself as social cohesion, the point in which every student in the prepared environment adopts genuine concern for the well-being and success of all his classmates.[351] This level of spontaneous peace and goodwill provides a vital foundation for peace in the world outside the Casa which can eventually lead to peace on earth.[352]

Hyderabad: Orient Longman, 2006. Print. Pages 146-148, 156, 218-219, 222-223.

[350] Ibid. Pages 146-151, 156-158, 218-223.

[351] Montessori, Maria. *The Absorbent Mind.* Trans. Claude A. Claremont. Vol. 1. Oxford: Clio, 2004. Print. The Clio Montessori Ser. Pages 212-222.

[352] Ibid. Pages 217-222.

Conclusion

Peace on Earth

Peace on earth begins with the adult who fosters peace in a thoughtfully prepared home environment by providing cognitively appropriate activities for holistic development and by setting a good example for her children to emulate.[353] [354] The foundation for peace that begins in the home continues in the Montessori prepared environment under the guidance of the trained Montessori teacher. Following the acquisition of normalization through concentration upon age-appropriate, freely chosen work in the Casa's uninterrupted three hour work period in conjunction with Grace and Courtesy, internal peace develops as a precursor to external peace.[355] The peaceful conflict resolution skills students learn in the Casa through Grace and Courtesy lessons and The Peace Table as well as the virtues naturally attained through normalization naturally lead to social cohesion in the prepared environment.[356] Social cohesion, the ultimate manifestation of external peace in children under six or seven years of age, provides the groundwork for peace in the world.[357]

Looking at the earth through the lens of the Montessori Method, it becomes clear that our world is in the collective stage. Like young children who are not yet normalized, various

---

[353] Montessori, Maria. *The Child in the Family*. Trans. Nancy R. Cirillo. Vol. 8. Oxford: Clio, 2006. Print. The Clio Montessori Ser. Pages 47-62.

[354] Montessori, Maria. *The Child, Society, and the World: Unpublished Speeches and Writings*. Vol. 7. Oxford: Clio, 2006. Print. The Clio Montessori Ser. Pages 12-19.

[355] Montessori, Maria. *The Absorbent Mind*. Trans. Claude A. Claremont. Vol. 1. Oxford: Clio, 2004. Print. The Clio Montessori Ser. Pages 182-189, 202-222.

[356] Ibid. Pages 182-192, 202-222.

[357] Ibid. Pages 218-222.

deviations both large and small abound. From individual personality flaws to personal grievances to centuries old grudges and resentments to ongoing war, the world is constantly afflicted with collective stage behavior of various magnitudes. When attempting to attain permanent universal peace, it can be tempting to resort to negativity by describing humanity as "vile" or "inherently evil." Instead of ascribing negative labels to individuals or groups of humans or mankind as a whole, it is far more helpful to regard the state of the world and its inhabitants as being in the collective stage. Unlike divisive, unhelpful labels, the collective stage implies a practical state of hope for humanity's future. Just like in the Primary prepared environment, the universal goal for humanity should be to transform our collective stage world into our normalized world, which can only happen through our diligent, deliberate efforts to create lasting universal peace with respect for one another. As a first step, The Peace Table and its principles should be the universal model for solving problems and resolving disputes. However, there is only so much adults can achieve through peaceful arbitration. Perhaps Dr. Maria Montessori said it best,

> *A great social mission that will ensure the child justice, harmony, and love remains to be accomplished. And this great task must be the work of education, for this is the only way to build a new world and to bring peace.*[358]

---

[358] Montessori, Maria. *Education and Peace*. Vol. 10. Amsterdam: Montessori-Pierson, 2008. Print. The Montessori Ser. Page 38.

Glossary

This **Glossary** contains a list of Montessori terms that appear in this book. Also included are terms not present in the text that may be helpful during a Montessori parent night or parent-teacher conference.

Absorbent Mind: a mental power unique to children six years of age and younger that allows for effortless learning; the absorbent mind is replaced with a reasoning mind when the child is about seven years old

AMI: Association Montessori Internationale; the original Montessori teacher-training program founded by Dr. Maria Montessori to uphold the high standards of her scientific pedagogy

AMI/USA: Association Montessori Internationale's organizational division for the United States of America

Analyzed Movements: the accurate and precise manner in which the Montessori guide presents a given manipulative or exercise to an individual child to provide maximum clarity in order to best facilitate independent spontaneous learning; by using analyzed movements, the guide makes it easier for the child to remember the sequence of her actions so that he may work confidently and independently following the guide's initial presentation

Casa: the Italian word for "house;" a Montessori classroom for two-and-a-half to six year old children

Children's House: See **Casa**

Collective Stage: children in the Casa who are not yet normalized (See **Normalization**)

Control of Error: a built-in device in many of the Montessori materials that helps children correct their own work without external guidance

Cultural Extensions: Once considered a separate subject in the Casa, **Cultural Extensions** activities included art, dance, music literacy, geography, botany, and zoology. AMI reassigned and integrated these activities within the curriculum, particularly into **Practical Life** and **Sensorial**, to ensure such exercises would not be considered superfluous or inferior to academic studies.

Deviations: negative behaviors children exhibit before normalization (See **Normalization**)

Director/Directress: See **Guide**

Erdkinder: German for "Earth children;" a Montessori adolescent program, usually located on a farm, for twelve through fifteen or twelve through eighteen year old students; a Montessori Middle School and/or Montessori High School

Expression: activities such as singing, art, dance, and drama are sometimes called "Expression" or "Expression Exercises" in Montessori classrooms

Expression Exercises: See **Expression**

Facilitated Conversation: spontaneous or planned teacher-directed conversations between guides and students about various topics presented in order to enrich vocabulary and bolster confidence in public speaking

Facilitator: See **Guide**

First Plane: a child between birth and six years of age

Four Planes of Development: the four cognitive development stages in childhood and young adulthood that are recognized by Montessorians; 1ˢᵗ Plane: birth to six years; 2ⁿᵈ Plane: six to twelve years; 3ʳᵈ Plane: twelve to eighteen years; 4ᵗʰ Plane: eighteen to twenty-four years

Fourth Plane: a young adult between eighteen and twenty-four years of age

Going Out: another name for a class field trip; more common in Elementary than Primary classrooms

Grace and Courtesy: simple skits performed by the teacher for small groups of children; these entertaining performances demonstrate manners and common procedures such as how to use a tissue, say "excuse me," unroll a rug, and so on

Guide: a Montessori teacher; the guide introduces lessons to individual children at the developmentally appropriate time according to Montessori principles and her observations of an individual student's needs and interests at a given time

Human Tendencies: motivating tendencies that are universal to all humans such as the need to be engaged in activity, communication, and the imagination, to name a few

Imagination: the mental capacity to take pre-existing ideas and combine them in a unique, original way; Montessori is highly supportive of this universal human process

Indirect Preparation: lessons given to children before much more difficult tasks are introduced; "How to Carry a Tray," for example, is introduced before the child does any work that involves carrying trays

Language: one of the four main subjects in the Montessori Casa; spoken and written language, singing, music, music literacy, and poetry comprise this area

Lower El: See **Lower Elementary**

Lower Elementary: six to nine year old students in a Montessori environment; sometimes called "Lower El"

Manipulatives: scientifically designed educational materials provided for children in a Montessori classroom

Mathematics: one of the four main subjects in the Casa; numbers through the millions, the four operations of math (addition, subtraction, multiplication, and division), and fractions are covered

Montessori High School: See **Erdkinder**

Montessorian: a graduate of a Montessori training program

Montessori Middle School: See **Erdkinder**

Normalization: the process in which a child abandons all negative behaviors and replaces them with positive behaviors such as kindness, patience, helpfulness, empathy, and the ability to choose activities and concentrate without adult interference or guidance

Observation: a formal appointment where parents and significant others may unobtrusively observe in their child's classroom during school hours

Parent-Child Days: usually optional school-scheduled days when parents and significant others may visit and interact with their child in his classroom after school hours to see what he is currently doing in class; also called "Parent-Child Work Times"

Parent-Child Work Times: See **Parent-Child Days**

Peace Table: a designated area in the Casa where students can peaceably resolve their conflicts and reach an amicable solution with minimal adult guidance or interference

Points of Interest: vital details in a given lesson that the guide draws attention to; example: a teacher might give a child the point of interest to keep soap bubbles confined to the table while washing a table

Positive Phrasing: the honest and respectful way in which Montessorians communicate with students and parents

Practical Life: one of the four main subjects in the Casa; focuses on art and practical life skills such as hygiene, coordination and balance, and care for the environment

Prepared Environment: a Montessori classroom that contains a trained teacher, a developmentally appropriate mixed-age group of children, and official Montessori educational materials

Presentation: a lesson that is introduced to a student or small group of students in a Montessori classroom

Primary: three to six year old students in a Montessori Casa; preschool aged children; toilet trained two-and-a-half year old children are sometimes included in the Casa as students

Second Plane: a child between six and twelve years of age

Sensitive Periods: intense motivations for the acquisition of order, movement, language, and the refinement of sensory perception in children under the age of six; sensitive periods are often called "windows of opportunity" or "critical periods" in non-Montessori educational courses

Sensorial: one of the four main subjects in the Casa; focuses on the five senses (vision, auditory, touch, smell, and taste) and their qualities as well as geography and botany

Support Staff: an assistant who has not attended a Montessori training course

Teacher: See **Guide**

Third Plane: an adolescent between twelve and eighteen years of age

Three Part Message: a clear, concise message that may be delivered by one student to another to stop negative behavior by stating the undesirable action ("You hit me!"), saying what the victim thinks about it ("I don't like that!"), and then telling the instigator what to do or what not to do ("Don't hit me again!") before leaving the scene and reporting to the guide what happened

Three Part Work Cycle: the organized, deliberate act of choosing available work, working with the chosen activity or manipulative, and then returning the finished work to its correct place in the Casa in its original condition ready for the next student to use

Three Period Lesson: a game-like technique used to introduce new vocabulary to Primary Montessori students

Trained Assistant: a Montessori teacher's assistant who has graduated from a Montessori training course

Upper El: See Upper Elementary

Upper Elementary: nine to twelve year old students in a Montessori environment; sometimes called "Upper El"

Variations: independent spontaneous discoveries a Primary student makes with a Montessori manipulative following an initial presentation from the guide

Work: a productive activity with which a child voluntarily becomes engaged following an initial presentation from the guide

Bibliography

Goertz, Donna B. "Did You Say "Sorry?": Seeing Through
   Montessori Eyes." *Parenting for a New World* XVI.2 (2008).
   AMI/USA News. Association Montessori Internationale, Apr.
   2008. Web. 6 Dec. 2014.
   <http://donnabryantgoertz.com/2013/wp-
   content/uploads/2014/12/AMI-Did-You-Say-Sorry.pdf>.

Horning, Kathleen T. "Children's Books by and about People of
   Color Published in the United States." *Cooperative Children's
   Book Center*. The University of Wisconsin- Madison, 19 June
   2014. Web. 12 Jan. 2015.
   <http://ccbc.education.wisc.edu/books/pcstats.asp>.

"Impressionism." *Britannica School*. Encyclopædia Britannica,
   Inc., 2015. Web. 01 Jan. 2015.
   <http://library.eb.com/levels/referencecenter/article/42220#284
   620.toc>.

Jones, Sanford. *Youth Opera International: Reach for the Joy of
   Music!* Youth Opera International. Web. 6 Jan. 2015.
   <http://youthoperaintl.com/index.html>.

Kohn, Alfie. *Punished by Rewards: The Trouble with Gold Stars,
   Incentive Plans, A's, Praise, and Other Bribes*. New York:
   Houghton Mifflin, 1993. Print.

Long, John. "The Technology Screen: A Compilation by Three
   Authors: Jumpstart Baby." *AMI/USA*. Web. 10 Jan. 2015.
   <http://amiusa.wpengine.com/wp-

content/uploads/2012/03/amiusa-the-technology-screen.pdf>.

Montanaro, Silvana Q. "The Technology Screen: A Compilation
by Three Authors: Television and the Young Child." *AMI/USA*.
Web. 10 Jan. 2015. <http://amiusa.wpengine.com/wp-
content/uploads/2012/03/amiusa-the-technology-screen.pdf>.

Montessori, Maria. *The 1913 Rome Lectures*. Ed. Susan Feez. Vol.
18. Amsterdam: Montessori-Pierson, 2013. Print. The
Montessori Ser.

Montessori, Maria. *The 1946 London Lectures*. Ed. Annette
Haines. Vol. 17. Amsterdam: Montessori-Pierson, 2012. Print.
The Montessori Ser.

Montessori, Maria. *The Absorbent Mind*. Trans. Claude A.
Claremont. Vol. 1. Oxford: Clio, 2004. Print. The Clio
Montessori Ser.

Montessori, Maria. *The Advanced Montessori Method I*. Vol. 9.
Oxford: Clio, 2004. Print. The Clio Montessori Ser.

Montessori, Maria. *The Advanced Montessori Method II*. Vol. 13.
Oxford: Clio, 2006. Print. The Clio Montessori Ser.

Montessori, Maria. *The Child in the Family*. Trans. Nancy R.
Cirillo. Vol. 8. Oxford: Clio, 2006. Print. The Clio Montessori
Ser.

Montessori, Maria. *The Child, Society, and the World:
Unpublished Speeches and Writings*. Vol. 7. Oxford: Clio,
2006. Print. The Clio Montessori Ser.

Montessori, Maria. *Creative Development in the Child*. Ed.
Rukmini Ramachandran. Vol. 1. Chennai: Kalakshetra, 2007.

Print.

Montessori, Maria. *Creative Development in the Child.* Ed. Rukmini Ramachandran. Vol. 2. Chennai: Kalakshetra, 2007. Print.

Montessori, Maria. *The Discovery of the Child.* Trans. Mary A. Johnstone. Chennai: Kalakshetra, 2006. Print.

Montessori, Maria. *Dr. Montessori's Own Handbook.* Mineola: Dover Publications, 2005. Print.

Montessori, Maria. *Education and Peace.* Vol. 10. Amsterdam: Montessori-Pierson, 2008. Print. The Montessori Ser.

Montessori, Maria. *Education for a New World.* Vol. 5. Oxford: Clio, 2005. Print. The Clio Montessori Ser.

Montessori, Maria. *The Formation of Man.* Trans. A. M. Joosten. Vol. 3. Amsterdam: Montessori-Pierson, 2007. Print. The Montessori Ser.

Montessori, Maria. *From Childhood to Adolescence.* Vol. 12. Amsterdam: Montessori-Pierson, 2008. Print. The Montessori Ser.

Montessori, Maria. "The House of Children." *The NAMTA Journal* 38.1 (2013): 11-19. Print.

Montessori, Maria. "Nature in Education." *The NAMTA Journal* 38.1 (2013): 21-27. Print.

Montessori, Maria. *The Secret of Childhood.* Trans. Barbara B. Carter. Hyderabad: Orient Longman, 2006. Print.

Montessori, Maria. "Some Words of Advice to Teachers, 1924." *The Call of Education* 11.IV (1925). *Montessori Article.*

Association Montessori Internationale, 2005. Web. 3 June 2011.

Montessori, Maria. *To Educate the Human Potential*. Vol. 6. Oxford: Clio, 2003. Print. The Clio Montessori Ser.

Montessori, Maria. *What You Should Know about Your Child*. Vol. 4. Amsterdam: Montessori-Pierson, 2008. Print. The Montessori Ser.

Prensky, Marc. "Digital Natives, Digital Immigrants." *On the Horizon* 9.5 (2001): 1-2. *Marc Prensky*. MBC University Press, Oct. 2001. Web. 12 Jan. 2015. <http://www.marcprensky.com/writing/Prensky%20-%20Digital%20Natives,%20Digital%20Immigrants%20-%20Part1.pdf>.

Stephenson, Susan. "ADHD and Montessori: A Case Study: Denise's Visit to California April-June, 1996." *The Michael Olaf Montessori Company*. Michael Olaf Montessori Company, 2006. Web. 14 Nov. 2014. <http://www.michaelolaf.net/ADHD.pdf>.

Mary Da Prato

Other Titles by Mary Da Prato

Montessori for You and Your Child

My First Montessori Book of Quantities

My Montessori Coloring Book of Shapes

My First Montessori Book of Land and Water Forms

My First Montessori Book of Music Notation

My First Montessori Book of Leaf Shapes

My First Montessori Book of Patterns

Starting a Montessori Business

Thomas the Squirrel

For a complete list of titles, visit the author's website at:
http://themontessorimysteryunveiled.weebly.com